DEEPLY

Umberto Pelizzari

DEEPLY

IDELSON GNOCCHI

DEEPLY
by Umberto Pelizzari

Published by Idelson-Gnocchi Publisher Ltd., Subsidiary Publisher Division of
CASA EDITRICE IDELSON-GNOCCHI Srl – Editori dal 1908
Sorbona • Grasso • Morelli • Liviana Medicina • Grafite
Via M. Pietravalle, 85 - 80131 Naples - Italy - Tel. +39-081-5453443 pbx - Fax +39-081-5464991
www.idelsongnocchi.it   E-mail: info@idelsongnocchi.it
1316 King's Bay Drive, Crystal River FL 34429 - USA - Tel. +1 352-361-9585 - Tel. +1 561-207-7132
www.manualoffreediving.com   E-mail: candotti@att.net

Idelson-Gnocchi Publisher Ltd. is a Member of:
• DEMA, Diving Equipment & Marketing Association
  www.dema.org
• FPA, Florida Publisher Association
  www.flbookpub.org
• HDSUSA, The Historical Diving Society USA
  www.hdr.org

This is a translation of "Profondamente"
© 2011 by Casa Editrice Idelson Gnocchi srl – Italy

Translated from Italian by William Trubridge

Cover photograph by © *Fabrice Dall'Anese*

PRINTED IN CHINA

For my wife, Irene.
For Tommaso, Niccolò and Giulio, my sons and future boatmen in my spearfishing trips.
For my mother, Maria, who in all the years of record attempts suffered with me, more than me.
For my sister, Stefania, for her constant support and helpfulness.
For my father, Gianni, for all that he has done for me.

Summary

The man and the sea

Free man, you'll always love the sea — for this,
That it's a mirror, where you see your soul
In its eternal waves that chafe and roll;
Nor is your soul less bitter an abyss.

In your reflected image there to merge,
You love to dive, its eyes and limbs to match.
Sometimes your heart forgets its own, to catch
The rhythm of that wild and tameless dirge.

The two of you are shadowy, deep, and wide.
Man! None has ever plummeted your floor —
Sea! None has ever known what wealth you store —
Both are so jealous of the things you hide!

Yet age on age is ended, or begins,
While you without remorse or pity fight.
So much in death and carnage you delight,
Eternal wrestlers! Unrelenting twins!

CHARLES BAUDELAIRE
(translation Roy Campbell)

Introduction

From the surface to 100 meters and beyond, headlong into the abyss: the pulse slows, the body disappears, every sensation is new and surreal. Only the soul remains. It's one long dive into the soul that seems to soak up the universe. Each time returning to the surface is a choice: meter upon meter towards the light, I ascend to reclaim my human form. I am often asked what there is to see down there. Maybe the only true answer is that we don't freedive to look around, but to look inside ourselves. In the abyss I am in search of my self. It is a mystic experience, bordering on the divine. I am incredibly alone, but it is as if I am bringing with me the whole essence of humanity. It is my human essence that transcends the limits, that merges with the sea in its search for itself, and that ultimately dives inside to find itself.

When I first thought about writing an autobiography I had a bit of a laugh – writing was never my favourite sport. And yet I did have something to say.

What I feel when I freedive cannot be described in words, nor even in thoughts. It is a unique experience of body and mind. And yet since I could never take everyone by the hand and drag them with me underwater I started to observe my emotions and experiences: in every training session I would decode what I felt and memorize the sensations, then after I would hurry to write them down, translating them into symbols on a page. Every time I reviewed what I wrote strong emotions built up within me, bursting with thousands of details. I let myself observe my feelings, which intensify and become transparent like a world of water. As this world fills me, everything appears to me with an intensity that is both simple and spontaneous. Now I can describe what I see in the depths.

UMBERTO PELIZZARI

A *dive into* the soul

THE SCUBA DIVER DIVES TO LOOK AROUND
THE FREEDIVER DIVES TO LOOK INSIDE

"I am calm, I am loose, I am relaxed." I have just lowered myself into the ocean from the platform at the back of the support boat, and I've already started repeating these words over in my mind. "I am calm, I am loose, I am relaxed." I have to convince myself that it's true, and so I repeat the words like a chant.

As they filed into the water one by one, the men of my team each gave me a pat on the back. They didn't say anything – a simple touch was enough to make me feel safe, and send a wave of tingles down my spine. Now the

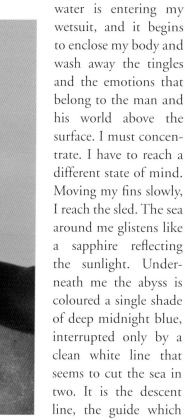

water is entering my wetsuit, and it begins to enclose my body and wash away the tingles and the emotions that belong to the man and his world above the surface. I must concentrate. I have to reach a different state of mind. Moving my fins slowly, I reach the sled. The sea around me glistens like a sapphire reflecting the sunlight. Underneath me the abyss is coloured a single shade of deep midnight blue, interrupted only by a clean white line that seems to cut the sea in two. It is the descent line, the guide which will take me down into the sea, where I want to go.

I feel alone and lost, like an abandoned child. Of course I need only raise my head to see that this isn't the case. The men of my team, the safety scuba divers, photographers, journalists, judges, friends, my mother... they're all here with me, only a few meters away. But I don't want to look up, I don't want to see anything. Everything I have to see is within me. I must not seek their help, I must not depend on anyone other than myself. Down there below, I go alone.

So I look again into the blue depths, trying to see down as deep as possible. With my

gaze I yearn to go beyond, though I don't know where. If only I could catch sight of my objective, but I can't. It seems as if the sun's rays want to help me – they break through the surface and slice conceitedly down into the abyss. They show me the direction, and invite me to follow. But I must stay calm – I'm not ready yet. I reach the sled, but before taking my head out of the water to climb onto it I want to look one last time into 'my' sea. It will be a long interminable descent, meter upon meter, before I win the challenge with the sea. I can win a contest with myself or with an adversary, but in a contest with man the sea will win every time. I do not defeat the sea, it is the sea that allows me to defeat it.

Now I am positioned on the sled. Again I repeat, "I am calm, I am loose, I am relaxed." I try and visualise the dive in its entirety, from the initial descent to the return to the surface. I see myself sinking down, as the dark water embraces my legs, absorbs my body, and overpowers my thoughts. In my mind I clearly hear the signals that my support team will give me every thirty meters. I continue down, and see the white tag there beneath me. I arrive quickly, tear off the tag and begin my ascent towards the light. In my mind the record has been achieved. Now I must prepare myself to go there physically. I must demonstrate to myself just how far I can go, just how deep my own ocean is.

I am concentrated on my breathing. I breathe in and out slowly, feeling my heart beat settle and my muscles relaxing further. My mind is focussed and my body is ready, and both are in harmony with each other. There is a mental barrier around me, dividing me from the rest of the world. I raise my arm and open my hand and the voice of Roberto sounds out, "Five minutes," breaking the perfect, almost pious silence that had been created. Now I cannot reconsider or allow any error. In exactly five minutes I must begin the dive. I am perfectly calm, and at peace with myself. I know that during the descent this feeling will intensify, but I must feel it even now, before I leave the surface. I cannot find serenity in the ocean if I haven't already found it within myself.

Four minutes to go. "I am calm, I am loose, I am relaxed," I continue to repeat to myself.

Concentration before a dive is everything. Even though the body is prepared by the months of training that precede a record attempt, when we attempt depths at the limit of our capabilities, relaxation is critical to achieving the objective.

I plunge through the surface of the water. The light of the sun weakens and eventually vanishes. But the sun is my friend – I smiled to it just before I sank into the depths, and it will return to accompany me in the last few meters of my ascent.

When I freedive I am immensely alone with myself. I leave behind any negative thoughts, affectations or terrestrial emotions. I must dissolve into the water and become one with it.

"Three minutes!" I open my eyes slightly and see the support divers disappearing one after another below the surface.

"Two minutes!" yells Roberto. I lift my head to look at him. We are friends, silent collaborators. I give him a wink, and he nods his head, almost in slow motion.

I continue to breathe deeply. As the seconds pass I become ever more relaxed, but around me the tension grows. I can feel it.

"One minute!" I put on my nose clip. I let my gaze fall into the distance where the sea meets the sky. Then I look to the sun. I feel its warmth. I know that for several minutes it will disappear from me. Where I am going its rays cannot penetrate – the blue is too intense, too deep. I smile at the sun. The smile is a positive gesture – I never begin a freedive in a negative state of mind, and so I smile.

"Zero!" I make the sign of the cross over my breast. I close my eyes, and slowly lift my hand. I take one last breath, as deep as possible. The moment my hand drops I feel the sled detach. The surface of the water crosses my face. I have

passed from air to water and begun to fall towards the abyss. My trial with the great blue has begun.

The first few meters of the descent I dedicate to controlling the sled that will accompany me loyally to the bottom. The brake is responding well, the angle of descent is vertical, and my fins are inserted comfortably into the cylinder of the sled. I equalise my ears for the first time. My body is responding perfectly, as it should be. I cannot allow any problems here, so close to the surface. If there must be exertion and sacrifice, and I know there will be, they are acceptable only at the end, when I have passed the present human limit.

The speed of the descent increases gradually. My mind is invaded by thousands of thoughts. Who knows what my mother is doing at this moment, or what she is thinking. Every time she sees me disappear below the surface she clutches at whoever is next to her, and whispers, "Goodbye, Umberto." I hear the first signal from Stefano. That means I'm at 30 meters. His is mostly a psychological aid. I don't need external signals

– my ears work like a precise depth meter. The body perceives, feels, and interprets.

"I am calm, I am loose, I am relaxed."

The sea is now a familiar blue, the blue in which I grew up. I'm about 50 meters down. Everything is perfect, and I feel serene. I keep on descending, and I smile at the thought that not many years ago hyperbaric doctors saw this depth as a human limit beyond which the body would be crushed, imploded by the pressure. Rather than imploding I'm thriving, rejoicing on the sensations.

Ivano's signal arrives on schedule. There's now 60 meters between me and the surface. I have almost reached terminal velocity of descent. The meters pass by in a flurry, but I'm not counting them.

I become at one with the water. I know I am a human and that I must breathe, but I feel as if I don't need to. 60 meters: even second world war submarines couldn't go this deep.

There, it's coming now. I have been waiting for it since Roberto released my sled to start my descent – it is the reason for every one of my dives. Every time, always at around this depth, an intense, indescribable sensation gradually fills my body from the feet on up. As it travels upwards it scatters any physical feeling: it's almost as if the body no longer exists, I don't feel anything other than my head. I open my eyes slightly, and look down. I see a pale cone of light that narrows to a point beneath me. The most thrilling thing is that that point is where I am going.

The blue is ever more intense, and my body slices through it. I am piercing the sea. Everything is beautiful, but I must prepare myself to confront the silence, darkness and the cold.

90 meters. This time it's Samuel who gives me the acoustic signal. I equalise perfectly. This is terminal velocity: three meters per second. I am hurtling downwards, and I feel my face squashed and deformed by the pressure. At this depth a force of eleven kilograms presses on every square centimeter of my face (156 pounds per square inch). The deeper I go the greater the weight of water on top of me.

The blue around me seems different now: it is deafening, intoxicating, powerful. I have to stay calm. I go back to repeating the mantra: "I am calm, I am loose, I am relaxed." I feel my lungs becoming still smaller. Even the heart beat is greatly reduced, but it doesn't worry me.

Now I'm in the world of silence and darkness, shadows and mystery. No one knows what happens to man at this depth. I feel pain and creaking in my body: the pressure is crushing my muscles and deforming my skin; transforming me. It's a good thing my mother can't see me down here in this condition! I would like to bring my right hand to the brake to reduce the speed of the descent, maybe even stop it completely, but a voice incites me to persevere: "Keep going, don't stop; now is the time to stop the man." It is the same voice that will one day tell me: "Umberto, enough!" As I listen to it now, so will I listen to it on that occasion.

I am mind and body. The body suffers, but the mind is stronger, and in this way the meters slip past. I must stay strong: in a few seconds the descent will be over.

Here the blue is inexorable, aggressive, and almost violent. I cannot make any mistakes. This blue doesn't forgive, not out of cruelty

Sometimes I yearn to stay longer underwater, at the bottom of 'my sea.' I have no desire to return to the human dimension. I know that these unique sensations will gradually disappear, but I cannot stop here – everyone is waiting for me.

The descent line and the bubbles of my support divers accompany me towards life, as if they were showing me the direction to follow.

or spite, but simply because it cannot. A sudden impact stops the decent. I have arrived. Conflicting emotions start to fill my mind. The first euphoric thought of "I've done it!" is immediately replaced by "Have I ever! I'm still in the abyss! The surface is impossibly far off!" My pulse is extremely slow: one heart beat every seven seconds; only eight or nine in a minute. My lungs are the size of two apples, or two closed fists: one sixteenth of their initial volume.

I must maintain absolute concentration. I have a strange desire though: I would like to open my eyes, look around and see what there is down here. Massimo always told me to never do it, as the ghostly surrounds could influence me negatively. But I can't resist. I want to be able to give an answer to those who ask me: "What do you see down there?" I do something I've never done before. I open my eyes. In front of me I see Massimo and Alberto, my guardian angels. They are alert, ready to intervene. They don't understand what's happening, why I've chosen to look at them. The pressure and the enormous contact lenses have deformed my face, giving it a uncanny expression. They are starting to become worried. Not being able to speak, instead I smile. I would like to embrace them, thank them.

Suddenly an intense shiver pervades my body. It is the first time I have ever felt it. Maybe it is from having looked my safety divers in the eyes. I feel sure that they too are feeling this emotion. I see the bubbles from their regulators rising upwards, as if they were showing me the direction to follow. I reclose my eyes. It's important that I find my concentration again. I would like to stay down here to experience, for as long as possible, this extraordinary, indescribable dimension, and I know that by returning to the surface everything will vanish. It is beautiful, but I must leave it – I cannot stay any longer. I am a man, and I must go back to breathe. Back there on the surface is a world of affections that are waiting for me… the sun and my mother. I go.

I leave the sled at the bottom, where we arrived together, and with long pulls on the line I haul myself back towards the surface. I grip the rope as tightly as I can: in my hand I hold my own life. The more I ascend the more I become aware that my body is returning to normality. I am moving towards life, light, and the air: air that I haven't breathed in more than two minutes. I feel like shouting out, "mother, I'm coming!" – I would like her to be the first to know that everything is going well.

The movement of my arms continues with regularity, interrupted only by a light kick of the legs. I hear the 70 meter signal, and I know I'm only halfway. Actually no, Massimo told me I had to always think positively, and so I say to myself "I'm already halfway there, I've only got a little left to go…" "I am calm, I am loose, I am relaxed."

Even though I keep my eyes closed I am aware that the level of light is increasing, the blue is becoming clearer, transforming into azure. I have to keep my mind occupied, preferably with something pleasant, and so I think about the sea, 'my' sea, its colours, its life: in the sea alone there are more colours than the brightest painting, more life forms than we can possibly imagine.

These thoughts fill me with peace, and in the mean time the meters pass by. The distance that separates me with the surface is ever smaller. At 20 meters I clearly see the sun that I had smiled at before my descent, and the shadow of the support ship's hull. I am completing the last few meters of the dive, and this is the most delicate and dangerous phase. I must remain calm. A sensation of intense euphoria fills me: it's almost as if I don't want to finish, I don't want to lift my head out of the water.

I would like to ascend more slowly, maybe even stop a moment, but the buoyancy of my wet suit prevents me. Abruptly my face breaks the surface of the water. I am back in the air. I could start breathing again, but I don't do it straight away.

The sensations and emotions that accompanied me during the dive vanish into the air. I have returned to my natural element as a terrestrial being. But still I don't breathe! I lift my head upwards, open my eyes, turn to look at the sun and smile once more. Now I can open my mouth and breathe in the air, but I do so very slowly. The first breath after a deep freedive is a powerful, intense moment, full of meaning that only a freediver could understand. From this moment forth I will breath a million times, but the breath I have just taken will be different from all the rest.

People are shouting, the many boats' foghorns are sounding, friends are throwing themselves in the water, helicopters, emergency boats… So for a minute I close my eyes again, stay within myself, and think back to when, several years ago, I would leave to go training by myself, in the middle of the sea with my little rowboat… maybe that was even more beautiful!

I make the sign of the cross. Before the dive it was to ask, now it is to thank.

The first breath I take when I return from the bottom of the sea is like the first breath I took as a newborn baby upon leaving my mother's womb: I will breathe a million times more, but this breath alone constitutes the passage from an aquatic life (in the abyss or in the womb) to a terrestrial life.

My name is Umberto

MAN WILL NEVER DIE AS LONG
AS HE KNOWS HOW TO DREAM
AND THE DREAM OF *HOMO DELPHINUS* WILL LIVE
AS LONG AS MAN HAS NOT COMPLETELY DESTROYED
THE OCEANS

Jacques Mayol

Fear of the water

The strongest, sweetest emotion I ever felt was when I saw my father, who can't swim to save himself, being kept afloat in the water by a wetsuit that some kind soul had helped him into, breathing hard through his snorkel, and with wide eyes almost filling his mask as he searched the hazy blue underneath him. My father, following the last few meters of my ascent from the bottom of the sea, wanting to be the first to embrace me and celebrate the new world record with me.

I remember my first ever contact with the water – the water of a swimming pool no less – as being pretty traumatic. At first my mother took me to the swimming pool to help with my physical state: I was small and chubby and had a heart murmur that worried her a lot. Above all, I was completely unable to have a shower: as soon as the shampoo ran onto my face I would start crying and I wouldn't stop as long as I was in the water. I had a hard time even breathing.

A doctor had advised swimming as a remedy, and so I was thrown into the local swim-

Two photos from the family album. From birth I was terrorised by the water. Judging by my reaction to the first time I was washed my mother would never have guessed what I would become when I grew up. As soon as the water started to run down my face I would experience an almost claustrophobic feeling and I would have great difficulty breathing.

ming pool at Busto Arsizio in the hope that it would at least resolve my fear.

I believe I have illustrious predecessors in this quirk of my infancy: even the mythical Jacques-Yves Cousteau was taken into the water the first time for more or less the same reasons; Dimitri Rebikoff became an underwater aeronautical and electronics engineer because he hoped to become a champion swimmer, but he had a one-in-a-million condition that meant his body density didn't allow him to float sufficiently, which is very important in swimming; and lastly Francisco 'Pipin' Ferreras, my friend and rival, started freediving in order to cure his asthma.

However my first encounter with the water had a positive effect: at barely five years of age I entered my first swimming competition, and soon after I discovered freediving. I loved holding my breath, and I did it whether I was in or out of the water. While I was doing my homework I would sit there holding my breath. The day of my first holy communion, when it is common to receive gifts from one's family, I asked my parents for a watch. I didn't care about the brand or how many different gadgets it had – all that I was interested in was the second hand, with which I would be able to measure how long I could hold my breath. Once, when I was in the third grade at school, already with a personal best breath hold of two and a half minutes, I decided to have a go at holding my breath for three minutes. Of course I had no idea about breathing techniques or hyperventilation: I would breath in and out very quickly, and as soon as I felt my head start to spin, and on the verge of fainting, I would decide that maybe it was time to start holding my breath. After two minutes my teacher noticed me sitting still at the back of the class, my face as red as a tomato, and she ran over to me obviously very worried: "Umberto! Umberto! Oh my God! What's happening to you? Umberto, answer me!" But I couldn't answer – I didn't want to start breathing again because I had decided that this time I was going to hold my breath for three minutes, and I couldn't possibly fail. So I rolled my eyes, gritted my teeth, and let out incomprehensible grunts and gurgles. My teacher was desperate. Finally I glanced at the watch one last time, started breathing again, and as pleased as punch I exclaimed to my teacher, "I just held my breath for three minutes!" My teacher could only let out the tension by giving me a smack that made my head spin on my neck. She sent me home, suspended from school for two days.

At home I received an even more severe punishment from my father, who never would have imagined what was to come twenty years later.

The funniest part of the story is that my teacher was born and raised in Syracuse, the birthplace of Enzo Maiorca, and after that episode she would always tell me, "leave all that to the professionals – you just think about your studies."

While my friends collected football cards I was writing secret letters to Jacques Mayol and Enzo Maiorca. They were my heroes and my role models. Freediving for me was a natural and instinctive choice. I stuck with swimming, and started achieving good results, but even then I would often hold my breath during training, as I did during class at school. I would wedge myself underneath the ladder on the side of the pool, out of view of the coach, watching my companions swimming lap after lap of breaststroke, freestyle, butterfly and backstroke, or I would even swim stretches underwater when I was supposed to be swimming on the surface. I still wasn't able to swim the entire length, so I would count the number of tiles on the bottom of the pool.

Despite all this I was still a 'pool rat,' living far away from the sea, and completely oblivious of real freediving and the effects of pressure. I didn't know how to equalise, or that the hydrostatic pressure had to be equalised in the mask as well as in the ears. Because of this, when I went to the sea, armed with mask, fins and a small speargun, I surfaced from my dives to 15-20 meters with swollen, red eyes that had been almost sucked out of their sockets by the pressure difference between the mask and the water. My father, the

At the seaside I preferred to stay safely underneath the beach umbrella with my little sister. To get rid of this fear my mother decided to send me to swimming lessons. Almost immediately I began a great love affair with the water.

sceptic, asked me, "are you sure it's completely normal?" to which I replied, "Of course dad, don't worry, it'll go away after a nap." I had no idea that my father's doubts were completely legitimate, and that in order to avoid the 'mask squeeze' effect I needed only to let a little air from my lungs out of my nose.

At the age of seventeen I stopped competi-

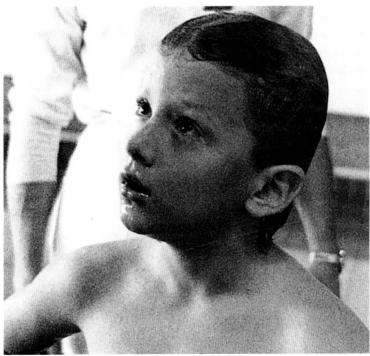

Only a few months after starting to swim in the Busto Arsizio pool I was already in the swim team for my club. I loved swimming, but my greatest pleasure was competing with my friends to see who could swim the furthest underwater.

DEEPLY

Here I am after one
of my first swimming
tournaments. I swam
competitively for
twelve seasons, and
I believe that this
was the best form
of training for what
would become the
sport of my life:
freediving.

tive swimming. The instructors at the Atlantis di Busto underwater club had noticed me and started to follow my progress. At this point I still treated apnea as a game: a different, personal way to experience the water. Then one day I saw a man called Stefano Makula performing a static apnea on television. My breath hold times weren't far off those of Makula, and with some encouragement from my friend Michele and sister Stefania I began training. I didn't have any training tables, not to mention techniques of relaxation, but the simple practice of two hours of apnea a day started to pay off. Michele and Stefania became a pair of slave drivers: they wouldn't tolerate a lack of desire to train, and until I had reached certain apnea times they wouldn't even let me out of the water.

On the 12th of June 1988, at the age of twenty-three, I held my first timid attempt in the swimming pool of Busto Arsizio to pass the 5'15"

In this photo I've grown up a little, and I've just set my first world record in static apnea. From that point on my mother's tears of joy and relief would accompany every one of my successes.

I'm proudly holding an amberjack that I've just caught. Spearfishing while freediving is one of my greatest passions.

mark set by Stefano Makula, who was already famous in the world of freediving. Even though there were very few journalists and photographers who followed my first official record attempt I was unprepared for the anxiety. In training I had gone past 5'30" several times, but on that day after just two minutes I lifted my head out of the water. I remember one of the official timekeepers remarking to my sister, "There's a big difference between five and a half minutes and two!" to which my sister replied, "If you don't believe he can do it then what are you even doing here?" Luckily for me someone pointed out to her that if the officials were to leave then even if I held my breath for an hour it would amount to nothing.

However after a few attempts I started to relax, and began to exceed four minutes. At that point I knew I would be able to do it. In the meantime the swimming pool had filled with spectators, more than two thousand in total, and when the large electronic display showed that I was over 5'15", the crowd erupted in applause, and I felt my first strong sensation of being a record breaker. At that moment I was still underwater, but I felt all the spectators close in around me. I could hardly wait for the 5'30" signal so that I could come up, jump into the middle of them and start celebrating.

Several days after that I left on my very first holiday outside of Europe. My destination was Cuba, where Pipin had broken the Constant Weight world record. He was my new idol: the man who had succeeded in beating Mayol and Maiorca. I quickly became friends with Pipin and his first coach Moro, and I could finally put my training and ability as an apneist into practice in the depths. I would go out with the Cuban fishermen and dive down to snare the huge Caribbean lobster beneath the *tableros*, large wooden boards the fishermen kept on the seafloor for the lobster to crawl under, and go spearfishing with Pipin at a depth of over 30 meters on huge reefs far out to sea.

It seemed like a dream to be able to spearfish with a champion of his calibre: the man that represented the present and future of deep freediving.

In the meantime my 5'30" static apnea record was beaten by the Frenchman Phillip Goasse, who took it to 5'50". The challenge was good motivation for me, and after a few months I reclaimed the record with a 6'03" breath hold.

However holding my breath in a pool was starting to bore me, especially after the experience in Cuba with Pipin, and I wanted to try something with depth. There was a problem however: I lived too far away from the sea, and it was impossible for me to train at significant depths in order to adapt to the effects of the pressure. Whenever I opened my mouth to speak about it, everyone would snort and say, "A landlubber like yourself should forget about competing with the likes of Enzo Maiorca, who lives in Syracuse, Jacques Mayol, who has houses in Elba and the Bahamas, Pipin, who lives in Cuba where it's always summer, and the young French men who are coming into the limelight." But I always believed in my own ability, even if I was unable to demonstrate what I thought I was capable of.

I was a good apneist but nothing more. I loved freediving, but was limited by the fact that I didn't live close to the sea and so couldn't train at depth.

1990: year of revelation

In June, as soon as I graduated with a degree in informatics, I chose to do my military service with the department of fire-fighters, in hope of being posted in a location close to the sea. If I became a member of their sporting club I would finally be able to start realising my dreams. On graduation day my professor, Gianni Degli, one of the most prominent researchers in the world of informatics and virtual reality, said in his speech to the new graduates: "I would like to congratulate everyone here, and in particular one of you who will no doubt eschew a career in informatics, and instead spend the next period of his life in contact with the sea. Good luck Umberto!"

I have stayed in touch with Professor Degli; he is a great friend, and loyal supporter, and I believe one of the first persons to understand the impulse that pushed me towards deep diving, and my desire to break the barriers of this sport.

Straight away I started receiving the first offers of work from businesses in the informa-

tics sector, but there was no way I was going to wind up in an office. My mother insisted that I go to the job interviews, and so in order to avoid an argument I had to become friends with the postman. His orders: don't put any letters to me in the post box – give them to me personally! In return I would buy him a coffee for every job interview that he helped me to avoid. "Umberto, I'm a human being and my bones are breakable," protested the postman, "How can I look your mother in the eye? Everyone's looking for work, and when they offer it to you, you look the other way? Mamma mia!" However he kept true to his word.

In the meantime I was asking to be transferred for military service to the island of Elba, which went against everyone's advice, since it was so close to home. The telegram arrived several weeks later and I was off.

The first stop was in Livorno. The superintendent was convinced that I was being transferred there for punishment: a fire-fighter from the city of Busto being sent to Livorno?! I arrived at two in the afternoon, and three hours later I was

A shot of me with Pipin. I knew everything there was to know about this legendary Cuban athlete; it was said that he had learnt to swim before he learnt to walk and that sacrifices were made for him to Olocun, the god of the sea, during a voodoo ceremony. When I met him in 1988 he was my idol – a freediver unbeaten in all the disciplines. The idea of going freediving with him was a dream come true.

confined to the kitchen to wash plates. There had been some great mistake – no one had told them that I was part of the Sporting Group, and that I was there in order to dive. That same evening one of the Fire Department divers noticed me in the kitchen and said, "I think I know you from somewhere." "That's right," I told him, "I'm a diver too, and I was transferred here so I could train, but the fax must not have arrived." He told me not to worry, and that he would talk to the superintendent tomorrow. Like magic, the next day I was summoned to his office, where I put forward my case, and within a few hours I was already on the ferry for Elba.

Upon disembarking on the island of Jacques Mayol's voluntary exile I knew I was far from ready for any kind of record. Difficulty, sacrifices, hard work and discipline would be required just to get close to the performances of Pipin, and I knew that the five months I had until the end of my conscription would never be enough. The most important thing for me however was just to live with the sea: for some-

A discussion with Massimo Giudicelli. With him I experienced the most beautiful moments, but also the toughest. Sacrifices and satisfaction, anxiety and victory. We started the journey together and together we finished it. He believed in me maybe even before I believed in myself.

one who was used to seeing it for three weeks a year, being able to freedive and spearfish as often as I liked was a dream.

I hadn't taken into account the superintendent in Livorno, who had given news of my arrival to Massimo Giudicelli, a diving instructor with the Fire Department, and a man who would leave a permanent impression on my future career as freediver, believing in me even before I believed in myself. Giudicelli met me on the pier, as soon as the ferry had berthed in Portoferraio. "I know who you are," he addressed me, "We will work together, one on one. You're going to have to pull your finger out, because we're not here to mess around." He had the stern, serious face of someone who doesn't smile much, and is reserved in their emotions. Tough, but likeable. I, too, felt he respected me already, but I made sure I didn't let on. He shook my hand with a firm grip and said, "We'll meet tomorrow and start programming your training straight away." Surprised, I replied, "I really don't think I'm ready to attempt a record… I think I should just train for a while." "Of course," said Massimo, "you're here to train, to increase your operating depth, and it'll be my job to make sure that you do it."

The training program prescribed my passage from an operating depth of 35 to 50 meters in five months. But after only six training sessions, between Monday and Saturday, the program was made redundant. With the rope set at 38 meters I continued the descent all the way to 50. Massimo couldn't believe his own eyes, and the afternoon of the same day he called me and said, "We should be doing something much more serious than simple training. Why don't you plan an attempt on the Constant Weight world record?" It seemed too good to be true… I hadn't dreamed of anything else in fifteen years. And all of

a sudden, from one day to the next, that dream could become a reality. After the conversation with Massimo, I couldn't sleep for excitement. Was I too going to enter into the "Great Blue Circus," as the veterans called it? Already I could feel the weight of a huge responsibility. Now the work would begin. At this stage everything was still a bit makeshift and unsophisticated. In the morning I would fulfil my normal duties with the Fire Department, then I would prepare our inflatable dinghy, load up the equipment, and when Massimo arrived we would head out to sea. On the rare days that we had an assistant on the surface Massimo would dive down to about half way and wait for me before accompanying me for the last twenty meters of the descent to the bottom. The depths increased gradually. We would dedicate the morning to training and the afternoon to media affairs, medical exams, and the logistics that accompany any record attempt. By evening I was ready to drop, and after a light dinner I would head straight to bed, but never without first having called my mother to tell her that everything had gone alright for the day.

At the time our team was a bare minimum.

Roberto Sparnocchia, one of my guardian angels in the depths. There is a great understanding between us, and we can communicate with a glance. A great friend under and above the surface.

Other than myself, going up and down in the water, there was only Massimo and Roberto Sparnocchia. Quality over quantity!

I met Roberto upon my arrival in Portoferraio: he was a fireman too and we became friends immediately. He was a team unto himself. Firstly Roberto was the ship captain, and the person who was by my side until the last moment on the day of the record; he was respon-

lines, adapting the boat to suit our needs, keeping the mayor and local council informed for the big day. Many of the firemen had never put their faces underwater, or didn't even know how to swim, but by helping out in these ways they all felt involved in the adventure.

One day a man called Adelmo Rocchi, a technician from Cyba Vision, arrived at the firemen's quarters to give me some special contact

'The Pirate' had an incredible charisma, and was one of the most expert divers I have ever met. He was deeply attracted to underwater archaeology, and would often tell me, "Umberto, as long as the seas still there then there's always something to discover." Maybe one day I will go to sea with him on his boat, in search of hidden underwater wrecks.

sible for the logistics on board the boat and managing any practical problems; even though he was a great diver he relinquished the opportunity to be in the water in order to coordinate the safety team's dives – he was the only person Massimo could trust with this position. When I gave the signal to depart it was Roberto who would unhook the sled, and at that moment he would hold his breath with me, resuming breathing only when I returned to the surface. Roberto has a serious expression, with a beard that covers his whole face, leaving only his eyes bare. But at the surfacing of each record dive those huge eyes would mist over as he fought to hold back tears of joy.

As the days passed, Massimo started handing out chores amongst the firemen at our quarters: painting the buoys, measuring and marking the descent line, filling old piping with lead to make weights for decompression

lenses that I had requested. He didn't find anyone in the foyer, so after having searched around a little he ended up in the kitchen. There he encountered a young fireman busy washing dishes, and he asked him, "I have some special lenses to give to an athlete called Umberto Pelizzari…" I felt like sinking into the ground. Red in the face, I responded, "Excuse me sir, even though it might not seem like it, I am the athlete, and the lenses are for me…" We both burst into laughter simultaneously. Now we are good friends, and we often remember that first meeting.

In 1990 the Constant Weight world record belonged to Pipin Ferreras, with 63 meters. I had reached 55 meters, and one day I decided to go to Capoliveri on the other side of the island to introduce myself to 'the Pirate' Alfredo Guglielmi. I knew of him from the articles and books written about Jacques Mayol, since he was the captain of Jacques' team. He welco-

med me, saying, "I've heard about you. Come and I'll show you around my place." He had a dive center which was also a kind of diving museum: old weights, tags used as proof in various record attempts, contact lenses, old yellowing photos of Jacques Mayol and the other athletes who he had trained with. I liked that place and its riches of history, and I returned whenever I could. One by one I met his collaborators, the safety divers who had assisted Jacques: Marco, Angelo, Jurgen, but most of all the mythical Gianfranco Carletti, who was only ever referred to by the nickname 'Water pump,' earned from working for years in the sewerage systems of Elba. 'Pirate' claimed that 'Water pump' was a genuine sea-dog, and the most important member of Jacques Mayol's team, as everyone depended directly on him: he knew how to anchor the support boat properly, how and when to lower the oxygen tanks for decompression,

how and when to resolve any problem or emergency.

'The Pirate' quickly cut me down to size: "A lot of people can dive to 55 meters," he said, "the problem is getting to 63." I continued with my training, and one day I returned to Capoliveri and upon seeing Gianfranco said: "Hey Pirate, I'm good for 65 meters now!" "Holy crap! I don't believe it!" he replied, "Tomorrow we can go out together and you can show me for yourself." So the morning after I found myself aboard the *Pirate*, the boat that takes its name from its captain, and which was used as support boat for all of Mayol's records. "You can sit here at the stern," and the Pirate laid out the legendary white, yellow and black blanket that Jacques used during his yogic preparation. I was overcome with emotion, and I gingerly sat down on that aged blanket, as if I was not yet worthy of using such an important piece of memorabilia. Massimo was

A picture of Jacques Mayol on his famous yellow and black blanket, during his relaxation in preparation for a dive. When 'The Pirate' welcomed me on board his boat for the first time he told me I could use the same blanket, but feeling as yet unworthy I declined.

at my side, and whispered, "stay calm, it's just a dive like any other." In that training session I reached 68 meters, returning perfectly to the surface. "In Constant Weight you're going to be unbeatable!" explained the Pirate, "but I think you would be good in Variable Weight as well." Though he may have already been thinking ahead, I was still thinking of the task at hand: I had to officially exceed Pipin's record of 63 meters.

Finally the big day arrived. The night before, the Fire Department was invaded by journalists, television crews, friends, relatives, and photographers who had to find out just who this unknown diver was. Roberto called me aside: "Get out of here, and don't come back until tomorrow morning." I knew he was right, and so I excused myself for a moment, opened the trapdoor, and slid down the firemen's pole to the car park. Roberto was waiting for me in the car, with the motor running, and we fled to Massimo's house, where I slept the night. The day after was the 10th of November, 1990. Roberto accompanied me to the beach. After that first day he would repeat this ritual on every record attempt. It's the moment of quiet that I need in order to clear my mind, and concentrate on the task ahead. Soon enough I was onboard the *Pirate* and doing my preparation on Mayol's blanket. Then I was lowering myself into the water, which was already quite cold, the surface ruffled by a freezing north-wester. I went down determined: 65 meters. The world record in Con-

(above)
On the surface after my first depth world record, on the 10th November, 1990. Just like a first love, I will never be able to forget it.

(left)
A Constant Weight freedive.

(right)
My mother was beginning to realise that my life might be taking a different turn to what she had imagined.

stant Weight was now mine. When I broke the surface of the water with my face and took my first breath, I recalled the words written by Enzo Maiorca in his book *A capofitto nel turchino* ('Headlong into the blue'): "The first breath that you take upon surfacing from the bottom of the sea is like the first breath after leaving the womb of your mother." That breath, heralded by the return to the human dimension after an intermission in the domain of the aquatic mammals, and stimulated by the joy of a sporting victory, my first great sporting victory, was a different type of breath.

I raised my head to take in the sight of all the firemen who in some way had helped me, loaded into a tiny boat at a distance from the descent line. They were celebrating, hugging each other, some were even crying: euphoric, they called for me to join them on the boat. But first I went to my father, my sister Stefania, and then my mother: I held her tight, kissed her on the cheek, and whispered in her ear, "Thank you!" They were unforgettable moments. In the meantime the journalists and photographers on the press boat were yelling and whistling for my attention: but who's listening to them! I was still popping champagne with my firemen friends, and since I'm normally abstemious you can imagine how that finished up!

Of course every record of my career had its own story. However the most jubilant was always the first: not so much for the athletic feat as for the atmosphere and the circumstances in which I attained it. And also because from the 10th of November everyone started calling me 'Pelo,' and from then on Pelo was my name.

Meeting Mayol

One month later I found myself in Paris, at the Nautical Tradeshow. In the booth owned by the magazine 'Océans' I met for the first time the man who I had admired for twenty years. Jacques Mayol was surrounded by a growing group of people clambering for his autograph. I became nervous, and my stomach closed over. When I was able to finally get close to him and introduce myself he responded with a smile: "I've heard about you! Congratulations! I really hope that I'll get to see you in the water."

And so started a great friendship that perplexed some of the people who knew Mayol well: in precedence he had never been so open and extroverted towards anyone. He maintained that he saw in me the incarnation of his ideal *Homo delphinus*.

I didn't dare ask him why. I hung on his every word, listening with devotion, and trying to understand the secrets behind his incredible performances. Jacques had a house on Elba, and would come to the island often while I was training for record attempts. I would go to him in the evenings and listen to his stories, feeding on his incredible experiences and his French cosmopolitanism. Born in China, brought up in Japan, with a wife and child in Sweden, Mayol had worked in a thousand different positions in the United States and elsewhere in America, and he had a huge popularity in Italy, where he set his most clamorous world records.

One evening the telephone rang and Jacques answered in a language that I couldn't pla-

In 1991 I met Mayol in Japan for an important international conference, that included the screening of documentaries on the sea. Every morning we would train together in a swimming pool on the top floor of a huge skyscraper.

ce. When he had finished I asked him, "What language were you speaking?" to which he replied, "Never ask a man how many languages he speaks, how many countries he's visited, how many women he's been with or how much money he has, because if he can give you an exact answer it means it's not enough!" His philosophies influenced me greatly, and not only those regarding the underwater world. He would often express himself or advise me with obscure proverbs. One day, as we were finishing training he told me, "When a man leaves for a foreign country he brings his wife and his he-

art, but he leaves behind the weapons and laws of his own people and accepts those of his host. You must be the same way in your approach to the sea. The sea is not a territory to conquer or a border to cross, it is a friendly and hospitable element."

He would often speak of his life and his relations with the other athletes of his time. I was always very curious about the story of Bob Croft, a formidable American freediver, or 'sea-monster' as Mayol called him, Croft was an ex-marine, with a lung capacity of ten litres. Mayol had a lot of admiration for Americo Santa-

Chatting with Mayol in his house on Elba. At sunset, from this house on the shorefront looking across to the island of Montecristo, we would often practice breathing techniques together. His teachings influenced my style, my aquaticity and my complete approach to freediving.

relli, a Brazilian freediver with Italian origins, who had outclassed all the pioneers of deep freediving at the start of the sixties. According to him, Americo was the greatest freediver of all time, a man with enormous potential, and Mayol was convinced that given the use of the new technologies and physiological understanding he would still be the man to beat.

But the most charming stories, which most sparked my fantasy, were those of the tribes and peoples who lived from hunting and gathering underwater, and who Mayol had visited in his years of wandering the many seas of the world: the lobster fishermen of the Turks and Caicos islands, the Ama and Itoman of Japan, the Pacific pearl divers. These stories would later influence the itinerary of my own travels: in fact, after having met Jacques I started dreaming about travelling the world, meeting new peoples and diving in faraway seas. I ended up following in the footsteps of Mayol, and seeing such places and peoples would always remind me of his stories.

So it was that I first left for the Maldives, to a little atoll called Felidu. And there one day, while I was freediving on the inside of a coral reef, I heard the sound of a traditional Maldivian *dhoni* – the fishing boat of an old fisherman called Brisby and his son. They stayed to watch me for a while, before disappearing as quietly as they arrived. The same evening, as I was fishing with a hand line off the end of the jetty, I noticed a

man coming towards me. He had the peculiar gait of all old mariners, moving on land as if he was still at sea, keeping his legs wide apart as if bracing himself in the wind, or finding his balance on a shifting deck. It was Brisby. "I saw you in the sea today. My compliments," he said to me in uncertain English. "I like the way you move underwater. I'm only an old fisherman, but allow me to give you some advice. Remember that there are two ways of going underwater." So saying, he took out a piece of coral and threw it in the water, then from the opened shell of a coconut he poured the sweet white liquid. "Look," he continued, "Both the coral and the coconut milk are now in the water, but the coral is still a piece of coral, while the coconut milk is a piece of the sea. When you dive you must not go against the sea: it shouldn't be you, your body, your skin, and the sea, no, every part of your being has to merge with the water." That old Maldivian, with his dark skin marked deep by sun and salt, who probably didn't even know how to swim, was able, with his simple words, his piece of coral and his coconut, to transmit to me the most invaluable piece of advice. A couple of days before I left, Brisby gave me a necklace of black coral, and as he hung it round my neck he said, "Keep it always with you, when you go down there into the depths. It will bring you good luck. Remember me, and remember what I told you." I would say that so far the necklace has done its duty, and as for Brisby, I will never forget the old fisherman.

It was in 1991, on my return from the Maldives, that my mother truly realised that my life would be nothing like what she had hoped or imagined for me. No computer science, no jacket and tie. Only the sea, and repeated attempts to exceed my own self, pushing myself ever deeper: not to break records for their own sake, but rather to explore my physical and spiritual bond with the sea. My mother was constantly worried. She would start praying every time she saw me heading out with my bag over my shoulder, even if I was only going training at the pool!

I left again for the Turks and Caicos, an archipelago south of the Bahamas populated by the lobster fishermen that Mayol had described to me. On those islands freediving meant peace and freedom. No animal represents these

ideals better than the dolphin, which has been considered a sacred animal throughout history. In the Turks and Caicos I came to meet Dean Barnal, nicknamed 'Dolphin Boy,' who was the guardian of Jo-Jo, a wild dolphin who enjoyed contact with humans. Dean suggested that I come diving with 'his' dolphin, an entirely new and exciting experience for me. We went far off shore, in the middle of the ocean, where Dean proceeded to shake an iron chain in the water – his way of calling Jo-Jo to him. I was sceptical, but after a quarter of an hour the little cetacean made his appearance. My heart was in my mouth, and as I prepared to get in the water I asked Dean how I should behave. "Don't pay

ted to warm to me, and after three weeks Jo-Jo had become my loyal and inseparable freediving partner.

Very early in the morning, when I would go for a training run along the beach, he would follow my stride, swimming close by, just out to sea. When I finished the run and dived into the sea to start a long swim, he would swim alongside me, at my ridiculous human speed.

Jo-Jo and I would often swim together to the neighbouring island of Pine Cay, where a beautiful dog called Tuffy would be waiting for us. As soon as we arrived Tuffy would throw himself into the water to play, and Jo-Jo, with his incredibly powerful rostrum (beak), would

Two vibrant images from the underwater world.
When I was still very young, and I put on a mask and snorkel to look underwater for the first time, I was instantly captivated by the colours, inhabitants and secrets of the sea. It has more shapes and colours than we can possibly imagine.

any attention to him," he explained to me, "Do everything as you would in a normal training session, and bit by bit he'll start to come closer to you." It happened exactly like he said, but as soon as I turned my head to look at him, Jo-Jo would swim off quickly, with quick flicks of his wide tail fluke.

I returned day after day with the sole idea to find Jo-Jo and stay as long as possible with him. To start with the results weren't so great and it seemed like he didn't like me at all. As soon as I tried to get closer to him the irritable creature would turn and leave me directly. I wasn't to be discouraged however: after a few days he star-

propel Tuffy (without hurting him) up in the air. After a couple of somersaults Tuffy would fall back in the water, and to revenge himself gently bite the dolphin's dorsal fin.

The friendship between Jo-Jo and Tuffy began long before I turned up on the island, and from the moment when I joined in they adapted straight away to the new company. Swimming with those two animals, or even just observing them in their friendship, gave me intense emotions; I felt perfectly integrated into their environment and truly free in the natural world.

Dean was adamant that I should not give food to Jo-Jo. He correctly reasoned that the

relationship between man and dolphin should remain purely that of friendship and loyalty, without motivation by any other interests. However one day I broke the rules. I was making a series of freedives along a part of the *reef*, when I came across a lobster out of his cave. I grabbed it, cracked it open and gave it to Jo-Jo to eat, as a reward for all the amazing experiences he had given me up until that moment. For the rest of the day that halfwit of a dolphin did nothing other than call for me, touching me with his nose, and indicating with his head to follow him, whereupon he would guide me to the entrance of a cave bristling with lobsters, in the hope that I would catch some more to open for him.

Jo-Jo quickly became very jealous of me. During my freediving in open water, when any of the larger fish such as barracuda, sharks or turtles came close to me in their curiosity, Jo-Jo would set off determined to shunt the unfortunate creatures with his rostrum, until his powerful 'head-butts' succeeded in forcing them away. He would return to me with an air of satisfaction, and look at me full of pride through my mask; then he would turn onto his back and would not resume his normal posture until I had patted him affectionately.

On my last day of training, the eve of my departure from Turks and Caicos, I was understandably very sad, and I had the definite feeling that Jo-Jo perceived my sorrow. After our last dive together, while I was swimming towards the boat that would take me back to shore, and then away forever, the dolphin pushed me with thrusts of his beak in the opposite direction, trying to stop me from reaching the boat. It was as if he knew that once I was onboard he would never see me again.

If someone had narrated me a story of this nature, I don't think I would have ever believed them. Nevertheless it happened to me, and afforded me an indescribable happiness. Fables such as this can become reality for whomsoever gives themselves up to the nature of the sea.

In the Turks and Caicos, an archipelago south of the Bahamas, I met Jo-Jo, a wild bottlenose dolphin. This experience remains the most beautiful memory of all my years passed in the sea. I never imagined that such a deep and lasting friendship and respect could be created between man and animal.

Here I am with Tuffy, an unusually friendly dog, and companion to Jo-Jo. The idea of a dog and dolphin as playmates seems like it could only come from a cartoon. Swimming with those two animals, or even just observing them together, was a beautiful experience. I felt perfectly integrated into their environment and truly free in the natural world.

The challenge of the deep

On my return to Italy I discovered that Pipin had failed in his attempt to beat my record in Constant Weight, but he had set a new record of 92 meters in the Variable Weight discipline (where the freediver descends with a sled, and ascends using their own force).

I met Mayol in Elba at the same time as the radio, television and newspapers were reporting the Cuban's new triumph. One evening at dinner one of the guests asked me if I was jealous of the fact that Pipin's successes were blazoned across the news, while my records passed almost unnoticed. Jacques immediately jumped up, furious: "I'll reply for Umberto! Jealousy for others is the first sign of one's own failure. Remember it well, Umberto, and remember all of you, because this is true with everything in life, not just sport."

As it happens I wasn't at all jealous of Pipin's success, which were in reality merited. Unlike the Cuban, I was only at the beginning of my career as a freediver, and there was still a lot of time to work on my public image. In fact his new world record only fed my motivation. I had returned convinced of having performed an excellent preparation, first at the Maldives, then at the Turks and Caicos. Now I began training again in the waters of Elba, with my mind fixed on what I was going to do, not on what had been done already. During that year Gianluca Genoni began training with me: his role was primarily as a safety freediver on the surface, but he began to gain confidence in the depths as well. With a long and lean physique, and standing almost two meters tall, his nickname within the team couldn't be anything other than 'Nano.'

1991 was the year that I had to demonstrate that I wasn't just a shooting star – I had to confirm my status and impose myself on the world scene of freediving. And that's just how it happened. Within the course of a single month I managed to conquer all three freediving world records. The path that lead me to these three records wasn't always smooth however. For the first time I was followed by a medical team, and for the first time we registered small problems with my health, which I was unable to perceive at all: the day before my first attempt a blood analysis returned extremely low values for haemoglobin, around 9 grams per decilitre instead of the normal 15-16. The doctors advised me to take iron supplements and other medicines to resolve the problem, but I wasn't at all interested. In fact, when the doctors in our medical team contacted a haematologist (blood specialist) for advice on what to do, they were asked, "So where is the patient, in bed or already in hospital?" Instead I was continuing with my training, and getting deeper by the day. Mayol encouraged me to ignore the doctors: "There are some things they are unable to explain," he said, "If you feel good then keep on going. It isn't just about the physical component, but also and perhaps more importantly, the mental factors, which science has so far been incapable of explaining." In his opinion I had achieved a jump in ability: there were many strong freedivers, but to be a record breaker you had to attain a new level, which could only be reached through psychological techniques that operate on the subconscious. Jacques believed I had reached this level, and so the foundation on which my performance depended wasn't physical or athletic, but rather mental. That was why, despite whatever problems the doctors had identified, I was still able to reach such great depths – I was diving using my mind, and according to Mayol that was enough to explain the results. His words gave me extra confidence, and after several days I was able to move the world record in Constant Weight to 67 meters. Then after almost a week of enforced stoppage due to the weather, on the 22nd of October 1991 I broke the world record in Variable Weight, using the personal sled of Jacques Mayol – a sled rich with history! I was almost scared of using the brake for fear of damaging that old antique! I took the record to 95 meters: three meters more (or less!) than Pipin.

The following day, the 23rd of October, there was to be no rest: I still had to conclude the triple with my training in No Limits. I remember the 23rd of October almost as if it was my birthday: with a dive to 102 meters, it was the first time I had ever exceeded the momentous barrier of 'one hundred.' On Thursday the 24th, I jumped straight from 102 to 110 meters. On Friday the Pirate and Massimo advised me to take a day off. On Saturday the 26th I was ready for the record attempt: I had to beat the Pipin's 115m, and I told the judges to measure the rope three meters longer.

1991 was the year of my debut in the sled disciplines. I finished the season having taken all of Pipin's world records. The 'Pirate' and Giudicelli were expecting me to have problems equalising at the bottom, but I was able to quickly adapt to the effects of the pressure. Mayol had taught me eastern techniques of breathing and relaxation.

When I surfaced from 118 meters below the sea, amongst crowds of friends and team members who were jumping from the boats into the already quite cold sea to celebrate my record, the contact lenses I was still wearing gave me the distorted image of an old man, without a wetsuit, who was swimming quickly with huge strokes towards me to give me a pat on the head. Laughing, Jacques Mayol embraced me and yelled, "I am 'deeply' proud of you!" I was only just beginning, and to hear those words from someone who had been the hero of my adolescence was an indescribable satisfaction. But the festivities continued, and between yelling, singing and champagne showers I paid for it with an eardrum… That's right, because I was no longer wearing my wetsuit hood when someone had the bright idea to throw me in the sea from the deck of the Pirate my head hit the water sideways, and I, who several minutes previously had descended to 118 meters and returned unscathed, ruptured my eardrum! The result was three months without any contact with the water.

In November of that fantastic 1991, during an awards ceremony in Milan, I had the occasion to meet my other idol: Enzo Maiorca. He was sitting in the first row, and I was about halfway back in the hall. At the end of the ceremony I stood up to walk towards him, and said, "Good evening, my name is Umberto Pelizzari… may I shake your hand?" to which he replied, "I know very well who you are, and I have been looking forward to meeting and talking with you!" That was how I came to shake the hand of the living legend of freediving. I guess I had been waiting for that moment from when, as a child, I would spend entire afternoons reading his books: *A capofitto nel turchino* (Head over heels into the blue) and *Sotto il segno di Tanit* (Under the sign of Tanit). They were beautiful tales that spoke of the seas of Syracuse and his experiences freediving there.

Ten years earlier I had attended a talk given by Maiorca, and I hadn't missed a single word he said. I liked his easy and involving way of communicating, like an old sea dog with tales to tell. From his stories emerged the presence of a sincere and virtuous man, and it was this that I liked most about him.

His rivalries with Mayol always excited me. I wasn't a supporter of either of the two – I believed their records constituted conquests not of other individual athletes, but of humanity in general: after any one of their records it was always freediving that won in the end. If I must be sincere though, ever since I was a kid I always felt closer to Maiorca, but only because he was Italian like myself. Jacques Mayol knew about this.

In the fifties there was a respected French doctor by the name of Cabarrou, a physiologist from Jacques Cousteau's team, who had developed theories on freediving wherein he stated that no human being would be able to exceed a depth of 50 meters without being inexorably crushed by the hydrostatic pressure. Enzo Maiorca couldn't have cared less: "According to scientific calculations, the bumblebee shouldn't be able to fly," Enzo observed, "But the bumblebee doesn't know that, and so he flies." So it was in August of 1961 Enzo descended without incident past this supposed barrier. One can only imagine how much mental control,

I met Maiorca in 1991. I had always admired the man and his performances, and I could never have imagined that one day I would be diving deeper than him. He came across immediately as a sincere and virtuous man, and it was this that I liked most about him.

(on the previous page) The ascent from a Variable Weight dive requires a lot of technique. I keep my eyes closed, and my body relaxed. Lengthening my arms, my hand closes automatically on the line in order to pull myself upwards.

Every freediver has a team of safety divers: a group of experienced professionals who work hard and make many sacrifices without ever being recognised in the annals. Each member has a precise and important role in the team, and gives me the peace of mind that I am diving in maximum safety. I would never be able to set a record without them, and we are bound by a great friendship and strong sense of unity. Here is the traditional group shot after a successful record attempt.

(left)
Immediately after a record the celebrations begin. I return to the water and shake hands, one by one, with all my safety divers who are waiting in decompression. Then I pass them a bottle of champagne, and we make a toast together – although the last to get the bottle always ends up drinking sea water!

(right)
Even though I am teetotal, I can't deny the contagious enthusiasm of my friends and supporters.

courage and conviction in his own ideas were required to fly in the face of what had been said by Cabarrou – a highly experienced doctor who based his theories on the current understanding of hyperbaric medicine.

After that first meeting we crossed paths several times again, but unfortunately I never had the opportunity to dive with him, or the time to talk at length about his experiences or listen to his advice. If I exceeded his best results then I owe it perhaps to his exploits and those of the others that came before me in the history of freediving. Progress in scientific and technological research indicate that those to come will dive even deeper. But no one will ever be able to become legends of freediving like Maiorca and Mayol.

Enzo and Jacques, with their contrasting personalities, stood at opposite poles in the world of freediving: Enzo was a great idealist, deeply connected with his homeland, with tradition and with his family; Jacques was a cosmopolitan, extroverted, and comfortable with many cultures and languages. What they did have in common was that they were both wise, courageous, and helpful.

In May of 1992, in Cuba, Pipin reclaimed the most important and prestigious record, Constant Weight, with a dive to 68 meters that exceed my record by one meter. I decided to

I was always fascinated by watching sea creatures in their natural environment. I wanted to learn their secrets. In order to be able to get close to them without scaring them you need to be able to move with elegance and aquaticity – in short to be like one of them.

reply as soon as possible, and I planned an attempt for September, in Ustica, where the Blue Olympics were to be held. Ustica, an island off the northern coast of Sicily, is the Italian diving capital: it is a marine park, and since 1959 it has hosted the International Review of Subacquatic Activity, a meeting of all the big names in diving. In the waters surrounding this island both Maiorca and Mayol had attempted freediving records, and amongst its honorary citizens Ustica boasted the Captain Jacques-Yves Cousteau.

I spent June, July and August on Elba, training with Massimo. In September we transferred to Ustica, and it was the first time that the 'Pi-

rate' had travelled so far from his home. Pipin was also present on the island, with his huge support team in tow. On the 17th of September I took back the record in Constant Weight, with a dive to 70 meters. It was another great experience, and an immense joy to be the first to break the barrier of 70 meters in the discipline I valued most. For the first time, I adopted the advice of Hugues Dessault, one of the founding figures of diving, and attached my weights to my wrists instead of around my waist. I used two lead bracelets, each weighing half a kilo, and this kept the weight concentrated in the leading edge of my body, helping it to remain oriented vertically, in-

trainer for Francisco 'Pipin' Ferreras, the second as the team manager for Umberto 'Pelo' Pelizzari. We attended the first meeting, myself with Massimo Giudicelli and Alfredo Guglielmi, and Pipin with Nuccio Di Dato and Luigi Leoni. Between Pipin and myself there was a certain friendship and sporting rivalry, and so the team captains didn't have any grounds for hostility as far as we were concerned, but 'The Pirate' and Di Dato began immediately to taunt each other, invoking the long-distance attacks of twenty years prior between Maiorca and Mayol! "You accused us of faking our world record!" "Yes, and I'll say it again now! But did you ever invite me to attend one of your records?" "Of course we did!" "Yes, but you told us the day before! How could I cover a thousand kilometres of land and sea between Sicily and Elba in a single day?" "That's not true – we gave you plenty of notice!" In the end the stern intervention of Franco May, president of the Diving Federation, returned order before the animated discussion could degenerate further. Those two men represented, with their ex-athletes, the history of freediving, perhaps in the most beautiful, pioneering era of the sport – both for the athletes and their assisting divers. Freediving rivalries had been their lives, and finding themselves once again on the scene to follow me and Pipin was a great stimulus for them and a new lease on life: head to head with each other just like the good old days.

This memorable match-up in Ustica came to an end, and after a brief period at home with my family, I left again for the tropical seas, with my first stop in the Bahamas. There I decided to join a group of marine biologists and sailors who were about to head south on an ambitious mission to conduct research on the state of a vast area of coral reef, that included the Bahamas, the Caribbean, the Antilles, Trinidad, Aruba and the Venezuelan islands. But since I was neither a biologist nor an expert sailor (the fleet was made up of three enormous catamarans), I had to convince them to take me on board as ship's boy, with the promise that I would spend the day spearfishing in order to supply seafood for the evening meal. I strategically refrained from telling them about my degree in computer science in order to dodge spending half the day typing data into a com-

stead of having the weight distributed uniformly throughout the body as is the case with a weight belt on the waist. Dessault had this bright idea one evening, while we were returning to Port San Domiano in Corsica, when he noticed that the buoy he used to tie off his boat was weighted from below by a small lead weight attached to its base.

In Ustica, at the same event, and for the first time after twenty five years of polemics and quarrels by means of the daily papers, Nuccio Di Dato, the ex-coach of Enzo Maiorca, and Alfredo Guglielmi 'The Pirate,' the ex-coach of Jacques Mayol, found themselves face to face, the first as

puter. I have incredible memories from those three months in the Caribbean seas: I learnt how to sail, to navigate and use a sextant... but most importantly I was witness to the most amazing things underwater.

In the early morning I would jump in the boat's tender and motor over to whichever point I thought might be the most interesting, and by myself I would dive into the water. There were spectacular encounters with the sea-life: caressing huge, seemingly aggressive moray eels, watching the elegant movements of scorpion fish, swimming with schools of rays and immense, peaceful manta rays. And more... barracudas, pods of wild dolphins, gentle manatees – the sea-mammal that gave rise to the legend of mermaids. One day, on the island of San Salvador, I had been in the water for only a short time when, during a descent, everything suddenly went quite dark, as if a heavy cloud had passed in front of the sun. The difference was that I had the strange sensation of being observed, and turning my head I saw, about half a meter above my fins, a huge hammerhead shark looking at me curiously. The shock gave me a sudden jolt, and I stopped my

descent. The huge fish, itself surprised by my reaction, started swimming off again with wide flicks of its caudal fin, and although I tried I could not get close to it again.

The biggest irony was that my shipmates would listen with great envy to the stories I brought back to the boat. They were diving exclusively with scuba gear, and the bubbles from their regulators would irritate or scare the fish, which would maintain a constant distance from them. For this reason many of them were eventually persuaded to try freediving! At the end of that trip, instead of returning to Europe I decided to stay longer and try to get to Martinique where I could start depth training.

It was there, on the 1st of May 1993, at six o'clock in the evening, that I ran the biggest risk of my freediving career. A party had been organised with a barbecue on the beach, and it was my job to supply the lobsters for the grill. A few days beforehand I had found a cave bristling with crustaceans, with its opening at a depth of around 20 meters. The cave, which was less than a meter in height, went back for about 20 meters. I had already caught several lobsters, but in order to get more I had to keep

(right)
A photo of me in the company of a giant Napoleon wrasse.

(below)
A manatee awards me a photo. These sea-mammals inspired
the legends of mermaids.

going back further into the cave, where the lobsters were trying to escape from me. The cave was too narrow to turn around, so to get out I had to swim backwards with difficulty. After about ten dives the water had become cloudy from my efforts, and at a certain point while I was moving backwards my fins came up against hard rock: I had inadvertently wound up in a side passage. I couldn't see anything any more, and I had no idea which direction to take. I made the sign of the cross and started with my right hand to feel the rock around me. At this point I was on my last legs, almost completely out of breath. Instinctively I started finning, moving towards an unknown part of the black water. Suddenly I saw a diffuse blue glow – the exit! Light flooded back in, and then I could see the surface again. I started swimming frantically towards it, and at a depth of about 7 meters I looked up towards the surface and saw the face of Feliz, the half-caste kid who had accompanied me. This was the last image that I can recall. When I came back to my senses I was already in the little inflatable dinghy that I was using for spearfishing, and Feliz was swimming madly towards shore to get help. How I got to the dinghy, or on board it, I had absolutely no idea. For two nights I woke continuously in a cold sweat, with the nightmare of being back in that pitch-black cave, tangled up amongst lobster feelers which were blocking me from finding the exit of that mortal trap. I have always loved to uncover the secrets of underwater caves while freediving, but after that experience I have become more cautious, and there are certain risks that I no longer take. In June of the same year, Pipin broke the record in Variable Weight by a single meter, with a 96 meter dive. I say a 'single' meter, not because it's a small increment at those depths, but because the year before he had tried, at Ustica, to take it six meters deeper, from 95 to 101, and unfortunately he blacked out during the ascent. I had two options ahead of me, from which I could choose only one: either to attempt to reclaim the record in Variable Weight, or to accept the challenge with Pipin in No Limits. I opted for the second.

For the first time I experimented with a sled that allowed me to stay in a head-up posi-

tion, making it easier to equalise, since the air in your lungs wants to rise upwards, towards the head and ears. During the first week of trials this new system gave me many problems. One day I reached the bottom and opened the valve on the air tank to inflate the lift bag which would bring me back to the surface, but the tank was empty; in another dive the lift bag itself detached, due to an abnormal rotation of the whole system during the descent; in particular currents the sled assumed an oblique position which made it badly imbalanced; on yet another occasion the brake didn't work due to a 'hydroplaning' effect between the rope and the brake plate, similar to what happens with car brakes on a flooded road. There was a great temptation to return to Jacques' old trusty sled. But within the space of a week Massimo and 'Water pump' had fixed everything. We had also transferred base from *The Pirate* to *The Shark*, a newer and bigger boat that allowed us to keep training even when the weather deteriorated. My training was as meticulous and severe as always. After a few Variable Weight dives, to verify that all of the problems with the new sled had been resolved, Massimo prescribed me a long series of training sessions in Constant Weight. No weighted sleds, only up-and-down over and over again with fins, until one day, after a training session where I reached 70 meters he told me, "Well done. From tomorrow we'll go back to the sled." Massimo affirmed, evidently with reason, that if an athlete was mentally and physically prepared for Constant Weight then he would be able to tackle the other disciplines with greater calm and safety.

The team was tight-knit, inspired and confident, but the weather would ultimately spoil the party. Day after day of foul weather forced me to do what no freediver ever wants to do: postpone continually the day of the world record attempt. On the 1st of October we had a press conference and the rope was measured with a mark at 123 meters. Everything was in place for the day after, but on the 2nd of October the wind was blowing at force eight on the Beaufort scale, and the sea was whipped into a frenzy, so there was nothing we could do. The same on the 3rd. On Monday the 4th I managed a training session, but the next day

I am always drawn to underwater caves, and love to uncover their secrets while freediving. I play hide and seek with the sea and its inhabitants, but after a terrifying experience in Martinique I have become a lot more cautious.

The last breaths before a dive to maximum depth are the most delicate of all. In this phase, whilst trying to maintain complete relaxation I attempt to fill every nook and cranny of my lungs. Down there, on the bottom, even the smallest amount of air is important.

it was back to enforced rest, as Elba was lashed by rain and squalls: it continued for Tuesday, Wednesday, Thursday and Friday. Luckily the discipline of No Limits is the least 'physical,' and requires mental preparation rather than muscular work: if we had been organising a Constant Weight attempt then after four days of abstinence from the sea I would have lost at least ten meters. During those days I accumulated nervous energy as my body became weaker: during the day I couldn't eat so that I would be ready for a dive at any moment, and at night I would go to bed after a light dinner so that I wouldn't have any problems in the morning. I would wake four or five times during the night

to go to the window and see which direction the wind was coming from, or if the sea had calmed. And as soon as I opened my eyes in the morning I knew that everything would be postponed again. Gianluca 'the Nano,' who I always shared rooms with (mostly because he was the only one in the team who didn't snore) would wake and look out at the sky and sea and I would ask him, "How's the weather?" He almost didn't have the courage to give me the

truth, but would reply, "It looks like it's another day off..."

My morale was at rock bottom, and I was a nervous wreck. Once again it was Jacques Mayol who came to my rescue. "You mustn't ever take your stress underwater," he told me. "You can't fight with nature. If a problem has a solution then there's no use getting angry, but if it doesn't have a solution then what good does getting angry do?" He was able to view it very philosophically, like an eastern guru. But he was right.

Finally a break in the weather. On the morning of the 9th of October, after five days of not having even touched the water, we returned to the sea for a training dive to around a hundred meters; in the afternoon the weather picked up, and the sea was choppy again. We waited for sunset, and at 7 o'clock in the evening, when it was almost dark, I decided to attempt a dive to 115 meters. The water was very cloudy from the storms of the preceding days. While the team made their preparations there was a strange atmosphere aboard the *Shark*, especially amongst the safety divers, who knew that they would have to spend almost three hours underwater in the dark during their decompression stops. We attached lights to the sled so that the support team could see me clearly during my dive. Everything was ready, but just as I was about to enter the water Massimo took me aside and said, "Pelo, don't do anything stupid – if you don't feel up to it, or if you're scared then let it go. Down there it's going to be grim, more than you can imagine. Unless you feel completely at ease, stop the sled and come back up – we won't think anything less of you for it." I nodded to show that I understood, and he gave me pat on the cheek: "OK, I'll see you at the bottom…" I entered the water and got into position on the sled. When I was ready I closed my eyes and gave the signal to release the sled. It was the most beautiful dive of my life: having left in darkness, I arrived in darkness, and I didn't register any difference in light or colour. The safety divers told me afterwards that it had been the most spectacular sight to see my sled piercing through the total darkness with all its lights ablaze. It was pretty tough for the two deepest safety divers, Marco and Stefano, who didn't

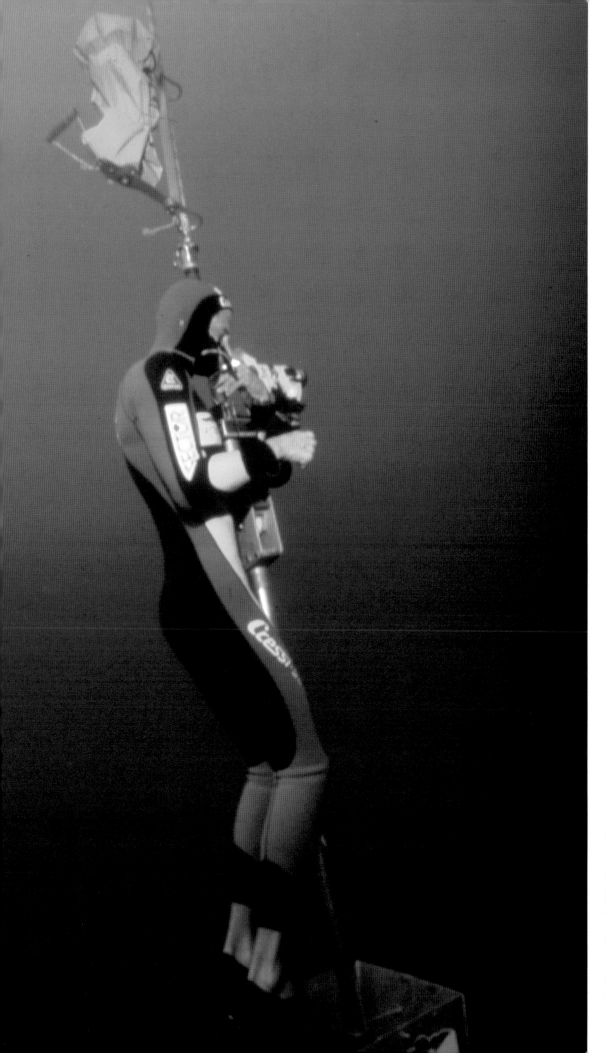

The No Limits discipline allows for the deepest freedives. The athlete isn't required to use any physical force – he is pulled down by a weighted sled (mine weighed more than sixty kilos, with a terminal velocity of three meters per second) and brought back up by a lift bag.

get out of the water until 10 o'clock at night, after an interminable decompression stop in complete darkness.

The great training result lifted my spirits for the record attempt of the next day. But the 10th of October was a day from hell. The south-easterly wind descended like a banshee, and the sea turned completely white. I spent the morning with Roberto, but not even he could lift my spirits. Every half hour I would phone the crew on board The *Shark*, which was anchored off Point Calamita, and where the team were all standing by with their equipment ready to get in the water if the sea gave the slightest indication of calming. But the news that came back was far from positive. Massimo tried to calm me over the phone, "Relax Pelo, nature is stronger than us, and there's nothing we can do about it. Look to the north and take a deep breath." He would often repeat these words to me when he saw me particularly restless or nervous, or if he was worried about me being too impulsive. In this way another day passed without diving. The same evening I called everyone together: the team of divers, Massimo Giudicelli, 'Pirate,' journalists, judges and doctors. "If I can't dive tomorrow then I'm going to call it off," I told them, "I know that this would mean throwing away ten months of training – the whole sporting season – but I can't go on killing myself with this hopeless waiting." That Sunday which my team spent in the middle of a savage sea, we came across the solution to the problem: on the horizon, underneath the lead-coloured skies they made out the form of Montecristo, high above the stormy seas, with it's lofty cliffs that fell vertically into the water, continuing for hundreds of meters below the surface. While at Elba, in order to find the right depths we had to travel several miles offshore, where

the land offered no protection from the wind, at Montecristo the same depth could be found a stone's throw from the sheer cliffs, under the protection of the island while the wind and waves crashed into the opposite side.

On Monday the 11th of October, at 6:30 a.m. we set off from Elba towards Montecristo. Even with the *Shark*'s powerful motors, instead of the normal two hours, it took us four and a half to get to the island.

My mother, who suffered badly from sea-sickness, wanted to be there at all costs. We had some difficulty finding an anchorage, but we finally managed to moor in the beautiful Bay of Maestra. Since Montecristo is a marine reserve it is normally prohibited to land on the island or swim in its waters, and so a patrol boat from the coast guard had been sent to escort us.

Finally, at four in the afternoon it was all over: 123 meters in No Limits. A new world record.

The exposure in print and television spread all over the world: two columns on the first page of the *Gazzetta*, the most important sporting magazine in Italy, and another whole page inside dedicated completely to my record. When I saw this response from the media I finally realised that I had completed a sporting feat that involved both dedication and complex organisation. These depths are reached in freediving only once an athlete has completed a long psycho-physical preparation, which concludes when he or she has attained a state of quasi-nirvana, inner peace and maximum confidence. The moment in which I unhitch the sled and let myself be taken down into the sea, I am completely certain that I will reach the target depth. I don't doubt for a second that I will take the tag from the bottom plate. But I know also that the unpredictable is always lying in wait, that at any instant my body might betray me without warning, and that I am risking everything.

(left)
Having arrived on the bottom, the last thing I want to do is leave it! Down there you experience unique sensations, but I cannot hesitate. I open the tank to fill the lift bag and begin the ascent.

(right)
Surfacing from my 123 meter record dive in the waters of Montecristo. The tension has been unloaded, and the joy is uncontrollable… I am once more the deepest man in the world.

The women of the sea

Despite my intentions to spend some time at home with my family, after just a few weeks I was already missing the sea intensely. I had been asked if I wanted to do a photo shoot for a Japanese nature magazine. I accepted on the condition that the photos were taken on one of the islands inhabited by the Ama fisherwomen that Jacques had often talked about in his stories. Even the word 'Ama' brought up exotic images of harmonious, poetic and seductive people. I spent two weeks in Shima, an area made up of jagged coastlines and enchanting islands. With the photo shoot completed, I decided to stay a little longer in order to meet with and dive alongside the Ama. These women live communally in their villages, and freedive for a living, following ancient traditions that date back to over two thousand years. The season for this practice was from May to September.

Originally the word Ama meant 'ocean,' but in modern Japanese the meaning had changed greatly: in reference to a man, it meant 'samurai of the sea,' while for a woman it meant 'lady of the sea.' Written Japanese has two syllabic alphabets, and around 1850 Chinese characters.

The word *ama* today is written with the Chinese character hai ('sea' or 'ocean') alongside the character *nû* ('women'), which are pronounced *umi* and *josei* respectively, but are read together as a single word, *ama*.

In the ancient times the Ama were religious figures within their communities, and covered political duties and the most important decision-making. Their way of diving has remained unchanged through the ages, and all that has changed is the equipment used: materials have evolved, and now the Ama dive with thick neoprene wetsuits so that they are more resistant to the cold. From their traditional costumes they have kept the white scarf, which they wrap around their head like a bonnet. Sometimes they even wear a kind of spacious shirt, like a poncho, covering their neoprene wetsuit with a white material that is almost like a religious emblem of their profession. Some say that the white keeps the sharks at bay, so the shirt serves as a form of protection: others give it a more religious significance, as a representation of a prayer to stay close to the god of the sea.

The Ama are divided into Funado and Okedo. The Funado dive with a technique that is a kind of 'Variable Weight:' they descend using a

Here I am in Shima, a small island of Japan. Together with four Ama fisherwomen we are preparing our equipment before a trip to the sea. These women live communally in their villages and freedive using traditional equipment and techniques that have remained largely unaltered for over two thousand years.

stone, and bring with them a basket in which they place the edible seaweed and shells they collect; on a signal their husband pulls them back up to the boat. The women would often ascend attached to the rope, bringing the basket with them, but at times they would leave the basket on the bottom and continue filling it during the whole session of diving. The Oke-do on the other hand would dive in a form of 'Constant Weight.' They would normally work in groups of five, and after every ascent they

Two images of the Ama fishing. They were astonished by my low-volume mask and by my fins, which were twice as long as theirs. They live in complete symbiosis with the sea, but it is an extremely hard life, and for this reason their numbers are dwindling.

Diving with an Ama
fisherwoman.
The white of the
garments they wear in
the water is supposed
to keep dangerous
sharks away, but they
are worn primarily
because in their
religion they represent
a form of respect to
the god of the sea,
who is hosting them
in his domain.

In Zamami, a charming island of the Kerama archipelago south of Okinawa, I made friends with an old fisherman called Terushige, a name that means 'rising sun.' He was a freediver also, and despite his age he followed me down for training dives. Apart from the language barrier, meeting Terushige was like reading an old romance of sea adventures. His tales and his experiences enriched my time in Japan, and meeting him taught me greater respect and appreciation for the sea and nature. As often happens amongst fishermen and mariners, every line on his face was etched into the skin by sea and salt, and held a secret – an intimate connection between Terushige and 'his sea.'

would deposit what they had collected into wooden containers that floated on the surface. Both Funado and Okedo used short, stubby fins and impossible masks, with huge internal volumes, making them very difficult to equalise – but this was all part of their tradition. My fins, which were twice as long as theirs, made a great impression on them, and the husband of one of the Ama convinced me to make a trade between my fins and his wife's worn out flippers, so that she could have my Cressi Gara's as a keepsake. They had never seen such an enormous pair of fins.

The Ama are a symbol of protection and good luck. They work underwater with deft and harmonious movements. I have had the opportunity to dive many times with them, and I have never seen, in any other freediver, the level of elegance and aquaticity displayed by the Ama. Their operating depth is between 15 to 30 meters, and their average dive time is over a minute. However there are no written rules or directions: their diving techniques are passed from mother to daughter, and it has been documented that in fifty years amongst their kind there hasn't been a single underwater accident. This demonstrates that their approach to the sea and their method of breathing may not be technical or scientific, but it is definitely efficient.

The Ama continue to freedive to keep their age-old tradition alive, but they are slowly dis-

appearing. In 1935 there were over three thousand, now there are only about four-hundred Ama. Once a year there is a festival in their honour, and there are daily rituals, such as the evocative liturgies to the gods with which they begin the day: in one of these they delicately hold a thin cord up to the sun whilst weaving an elaborate knot. They always throw something into the sea before they get into the water, a flower, a coin, a sweet, or a handful of rice, in order to request protection from the gods for that day of fishing. But all this appreciation cannot overlook the fact that these women carry out an extremely gruelling job. Recently some men have tried to take on the role, mostly concentrating on the collection of molluscs, but traditions, especially in Japan, are taken to the grave.

Today the youngest Ama is thirty five, and the oldest, at the age of seventy, continues to shuttle between the surface and the bottom of the sea. They told me that in principle, and up until recently, girls were initiated in the art of breath hold diving at the age of fourteen.

At the end of the day the Ama return to their little huts on the shore, light a fire, and together thank the gods for the protection given to them during that day. Then they eat some of the shellfish that they harvested. I was given the honour of being invited to one of these banquets, and it was a very special experience. At a certain point they stopped their traditional songs, and asked me to sing an Italian song for them. I was fairly sure that they wouldn't know the difference between a northern and southern Italian accent, so I ran the risk of singing for them 'O sole mio,' a Neapolitan song. As it happens I was a big hit, because they already knew the tune!

After this incredible holiday in the company of the Ama, I decided it was time for me to start training seriously again, and so I transferred to the south of Japan, to the island of Zamami in the archipelago of Kerama, several miles south of Okinawa.

At Zamami I would spend most of the day with an old fisherman called Terushige, a name that meant 'rising sun.' He was a freediver too, and despite his age he would follow me during my training dives. He spoke a strange dialect, incomprehensible even to the Japanese of Osaka and Tokyo, but we were still able to communicate marvellously, with expressive waiving of the arms, something that we Italians are particularly good at. The rare times when it was completely impossible to understand one another he would use a finger in the sand or a knife scratched across the wood of the boat in order to 'draw' his message to me. He was really an incredible man: of his seventy years he had spent sixty five freediving for seafood. He had a strange way of looking continuously out to sea: wherever he was, his eyes would slowly sweep the horizon, as if watching for an arriving ship, an island, a lighthouse, the fin of a shark, or simply the point where the sun would set. He taught me to recognise the details that escape less trained eyes: to perceive the slight changes in the colour of the sea or the form of the waves, and to listen to the subtle noises of the wind. I had thought that I was already adept at these things, but Terushige showed me that I had experienced the sea mainly from the coast, and navigating it was something completely different.

After these experiences in Japan I returned to Italy and began preparing a new trip to the Maldives, mostly because I wanted to see Brisby again, the fisherman who had taught me to identify with the sea. It was the 29th of March 1994, and I was gathering my things together when I received a telephone call from France with terrible news: "Cyril disappeared during training. His lift bag came back up, but he was nowhere to be found…" I was dazed by grief, shocked and in disbelief. Cyril was a close friend and talented freediver. Only the day before, an Italian journalist who was preparing an article on Cyril had called me to ask what I thought of him. I hadn't hesitated in replying, "Cyril is the strongest. In my opinion he's stronger than either me or Pipin, and he will soon replace Jacques Mayol in the hearts of the French." I left for the Maldives anyway, but with a heavy heart. The accident which had cost Cyril his life struck me in the depths of my soul. For a while I thought about giving it all up, stopping freediving forever, but then I realised that Cyril would not have approved this choice: he died looking for a way to surpass human limits and

the world records of myself and Pipin, and his death was undoubtedly due to a fatal error of organisation during his last training session. I owed it to him to keep on going.

The competitive season began again, and this time I changed islands: no longer Elba, who had seen my birth as a deep freediver, but now Sardinia. This island is a paradise for Mediterranean divers, and although it had given birth to great champions and the legends of the corallari (coral divers), it had still never been host to a grand sporting event like a freediving world record attempt. Sardinians are a marvellous people, respectful, hospitable and full of warmth, and I soon found myself at my ease. My goal was to take back the world record in Variable Weight with a dive to 101 meters. It would be a symbolic depth, since it equalled the depth Enzo Maiorca had reached in 1988, ascending with the use of an inflatable wetsuit, but according to the rules of Variable Weight I

would now have to reach the surface completely under the power of my own arms and legs.

Everything went perfectly, including a period of beautiful weather. On the 26th of July I surfaced in an explosion of bubbles and uncontrollable joy. But it wasn't a victory like all the others. In the press conference I said, "I would like to dedicate this record to Cyril Isoardi. He was twenty four years old, and my friend, but he would have been the one to beat this year. The sea took him away while he was training. Today it was as if Cyril was diving with me." His memory had accompanied me during the training sessions, and during the descent and ascent of the record attempt from the moment in which I made the sign of the cross, as I always do before a freedive. The day after, Cyril's mother, Mrs. Isoardi, sent me a heartfelt fax, in which she thanked me for the dedication, and finished with the words, "Be careful Umberto…"

An enforced break

Cyril's mother was right in warning me. That 101 meter dive filled me with euphoria, confidence and the feeling that I could attempt any depth. But on the 22nd of September, as I was training for a 130 meter No Limits dive, something happened that brought me straight back to earth. I was ascending with a lift bag that had a new design and was a lot quicker. I had only just climbed on board the support boat when one of my legs became paralysed. For all of three hours it was impossible for me to move the limb, after which its mobility gradually returned. It appeared to be a localised case of decompression sickness, an extremely rare, but not unknown condition amongst freedivers, especially those who dive regularly to great depths: it had been documented several years earlier by Bruno Vailati amongst a group of Polynesian pearl divers. We began doctor's appointments and tests immediately, and after we had been bounced between several specialists the conclusion was that I hadn't suffered an embolism, but rather

a simple rupture of a cerebral capillary, due to the violent increase of blood pressure during the exceptionally fast ascent.

The competitive season was over for me. The doctors had prescribed four months of strict rest, and no diving for at least one hundred days. It was a period that I would rather forget. I missed the countries I had travelled to, the open spaces, the colours I had become accustomed to, and swimming with Jo-Jo. My thoughts started to wear me down.

I was reminded of Brisby, the old Maldivian fisherman, as well as the words of my coach Massimo: "Remember that you can only go as deep as the sea lets you go. Don't become conceited, and don't be disheartened either – always stay focussed." And then there were the whispering voices after the accident, people who said that after that setback I would never be the same, either physically or mentally. In short, many people thought my record-breaking career was kaput. This gossip irritated me and I was unable to take my mind off it. I wanted to throw myself at once into the sea and prove myself again, but I wouldn't be able to until those interminable months had passed. So what could I do? As Massimo said, look to the North and take a deep breath…

My friends, those who were true to me, were aware that it was a difficult time for me, and they tried everything to boost my morale, but even they had to struggle to contain a deep anger for what was being said. Nevertheless they continued to believe in me, and perhaps I was the only one to really doubt myself. Despite all this it was during this difficult period of my sporting career that I had a beautiful experience, something which made me feel truly proud of myself and what I had accomplished in those years. A friend of mine who taught physical education within the San Vittore prison in Milan, and who worked specifically with drug addicts, called me one day and invited me to speak to the youths about my life, my sporting career and my experiences underwater.

I had already participated in conferences and debates, but always with a public made up of mostly divers, and with topics that were only ever technical. It scared me a little to think of standing up in front of young offenders with truly serious problems and who may have never even put their heads underwater, however it was a new experience and I decided to go. So one cloudy morning in December I found myself being conducted through the many gates and control posts of the penitentiary.

Cyril Isoardi, who disappeared at the age of twenty four during a training session. Like me, Cyril started off with a trusted group of small people around him: his faithful surface safety freediver Jean-Paul and a few others. He learnt yoga from Georges Orosco, the same instructor who taught Jacques Mayol. They told me that he was easily reaching depths around 130 meters. He would have been the competitor to beat, but the sea took him away.

His death affected me deeply, because as well as being my friend he was an open and friendly man.

My friend the teacher and the prison psychologist accompanied me, and we made our way to a wide corridor, at the back of which a projector and video player had been prepared so that I could show my videos. After a short wait about two hundred youths were escorted into the space and sat down in front of me. My heart was beating wildly, and with a lump in my throat I began to speak. I became aware, with satisfaction, that the interest of my audience was gradually increasing. Between the films, the odd joke, and some technical details, I tried to give them the message that what I had attained I'd had a strong desire for, and worked hard to achieve, and that behind the few minutes of the video there were long months of sacrifices and hard training. Little by little the barrier that separated us dissolved, and they accepted me as a friend. What I gave them was advice from a guy like one of them, not orders from an instructor. At the end of the talk I showed the film of my 123 meter record. When it finished everyone stood up from their chairs and applauded me warmly. Afterwards one of the prisoners approached me, shook my hand, and with a timid voice he said, "Thank you! If you were able to come back from 123 meters, then I too will be able to get out from the hell that I am in at this moment." Then he turned and left.

An intense shiver passed through my body as I watched him walk down that grey corridor and disappear at the far end. In my life I have taught many people to dive, and I have helped many others overcome a fear of the water, but never before in my life had I felt so helpful for someone. When that youth got out of prison he left drugs behind him, got a job and started a family, but the most beautiful thing for me was that he named his first child Umberto, after me.

Finally the four months of convalescence came to an end. I had a strong desire to freedive, but at the same time I was held back by a fear that the same problem might recur. I certainly couldn't dive in that state of mind, and so one day I decided to make a decision inside myself: "Pelo, you can either return to freediving with passion and confidence, and with your mind free of negative thoughts, or you can truly give it all up. Only you can know what you want." I decided to return to training, but to do so far away from everyone and everything: I didn't want to hear anyone's opinion – I had to be alone with myself.

So I took a flight and transferred to the other side of the world, on a tiny island in Polynesia. I was anxious to freedive, and I didn't want to lose any time – even before I had found accommodation I was already in the water. Gradually I started to come back to myself. It was beautiful, and it felt like I was being reborn. Finally I could see my colours, my blue, and most of all feel the unique sensations and emotions of immersion. At the end of each dive I would run

an inventory of my body and check that everything was perfect, from my toes to the hairs on my head. I realised that I was returning to the Pelo of old: during the descents I started to feel once more the strong pull towards the depths that I knew so well, and which had accompanied me in every freedive.

The fear was vanishing. With fear there will always be a psychological limit beyond which you can never pass – at a certain depth you turn and just come back to the surface. I was experiencing the opposite effect, and every day I wanted to go a little deeper. The abyss and its colours began to draw me in again, and the rapture of the depth was back: I was healed.

Diving in a sunken wreck is a special experience. Wrecks sometimes seem to come alive, and tell their stories to you, but in the silence and dark of their empty rooms I am able to dive into and listen to myself. After the accident of September 22, 1994, which forced me to take four months of complete rest, that's exactly what I needed in order to determine that I was fully healed and could return to the records.

The call of the Great Blue

THE DOLPHINS NEVER FORGOT THAT THEY HAD
BEEN MEN, AND IN THEIR SOULS THEY HELD
THIS MEMORY

Oppian of Syria (3rd century AD)

A photo of my team about to position themselves along the descent line. After the accident I would often look at this photo wistfully – I didn't know if I would be able to return to the water. But my safety divers called me continually, saying, "Next year we'll begin again with a new adventure." And that's exactly how it happened.

Villasimius 1995: return to world records

Upon my return to Italy I went straight to Elba, where I met with Massimo. He could tell straight away that I had definitely left the sad period of the accident behind me.

The final phase of training for the new season began. In July of 1995 I was back in Sardinia, the island that had brought me good luck the year before: my objective was the world record in both Constant Weight and Variable Weight.

The organisation was by now gigantic: as a base we were using the ship *Anfitrite*, which was on loan to us from the petrol company Agip; there were a good thirteen television crews, one of which came all the way from Japan, and at least fifty photographers and journalists.

In Sardinia I felt physically well-prepared and mentally very confident. Training was going extremely well, and the night before the Constant Weight attempt I decided on a depth of 72 meters. Since 1990 the record in this discipline had always been mine, other than for a brief period of three months. The depth of

70 meters had stood since September 1992, despite several attempts to break it, mostly by French and Cuban freedivers.

The night before the attempt I slept very well. Waking at 7:30 I went to mass, then straight after did some yoga and had a massage with Roberto. The transfer boat was waiting for us at the port at 1pm, fifteen minutes later I was already putting on my equipment: a three millimeter smooth skin wetsuit, carbon fibre fins, contact lenses and two half-kilo lead bracelets, then I was away.

I committed a serious error however: as I was taking my last breath and starting the duck-dive I swallowed some water instead of filling my lungs completely. In a fraction of a second I made the decision to continue anyway instead of resurfacing, in the fear of losing my concentration completely. There were two main consequences of that inexcusable mistake: a much greater descent speed, and at the bottom a difficulty equalising close to the plate due to the reduced quantity of air in my lungs. Despite this I was able to grab the tag, complete my turn, and without losing concentration start off towards the surface.

In July 1995 I started diving again. Here I am on the surface in the waters of Villasimius, Sardinia, concentrating and preparing for a dive, while above water onboard the *Anfitrite* the engine of organisation is in full force.

At 35 meters I heard Stefano's signal: it was like an extra mouthful of air, or a shot in the arm, and I started to realise that everything was going to be alright. Then came the surfacing, and an explosion of joy: the world record in Constant Weight, my preferred discipline, had passed from 70 to 72 meters, with a dive time of 2'02".

Straight away the water around me became a turmoil of people. In order to remove the lead bracelets I naturally had to take my watch off first. I passed it to someone on the boat, I have no idea who, and the watch disappeared into thin air. I wouldn't say it was stolen, but it was definitely taken away from me somehow. My team tried to console me, saying, "What do you care? It's not like your sponsors aren't going to send you a new watch!" But that watch was my lucky charm – my world record watch.

The problem at that point became maintaining the focus, as the season was not over,

meters, with daily increments of five meters, and on Friday I did a light training dive to 80 meters. Everything was perfect. I felt especially fit, and I asked for the line to be measured to 105 – I wanted to increase the Variable Weight record by four meters, from the current record of 101. 105 is a historical depth, since it was the last world record of Jacques Mayol: twelve years earlier he had returned with a balloon from that depth which I planned on returning from with fins or pulling on the line.

It definitely wasn't going to be a walk in the park, and for that reason both myself and many of my team were pretty tense on the morning of the attempt. From the moment I entered the water all of this passed, and after two easy warm-up freedives to twenty meters I climbed onto the weighted sled to begin the record attempt. I clearly heard my boat master, Roberto, counting down the minutes: five, four, three,

The dive site prepared for my return to record attempts.

and I still had to make a Variable Weight attempt. So the very next day I got back in the water for my first dive with the sled.

The physical preparation for Constant Weight was more than sufficient, but I still had to adapt to the pressure, train my equalising and then increase my operating depth. From Monday to Thursday I passed from 90 to 105

two,… zero. 2'40" later I was back on the surface with a world record in Variable Weight of 105 meters. It was the 22nd of July, 1995.

Having completed the season I found myself back on the island of Elba, at Lacona with Renzo Mazzari, the three-time world champion in spearfishing, and Angelo Azzinari, a passionate teacher of freediving. Together we decided

to create the Apnea Academy. We envisioned a freediving school that offered something new, something that had never been done before. We wanted it to have a modern teaching method derived from the experience of freediving and spearfishing world champions who were in the water for eight hours a day. The approach had to be more practical than theoretical, with instructors who spent their days around the sea, and who understood how to breathe, how to relax, and which training techniques to use. It was the first attempt to propose techniques for voluntary breath hold that moved away from the current methods, and were based principally on breathing and relaxation.

I spent most of the second half of 1995 and the first few months of 1996 in the Red Sea. I knew relatively little about it, so I chose the areas that I had heard were the best, in the south of Egypt: Zabargad, the island of green rocks – delicate olivine crystals; Rocky Island, with its sheer cliffs that disappear into the blue of the deepest water; The Brothers, twin islands sixty eight miles southeast of Hurghada, and held above the abyss by a flaming crown of spectacular reef. Then there was Sudan, which I remember most of all for the sea of Sha'ab er-Rumi, densely populated by grey reef sharks, *Carcharhinus amblyrhynchos*. Here in 1963 Captain Jacques Cousteau

The deck on board the support boat, with all the divers' equipment spread out. The men that ensure my safety breathe a special mix of helium, oxygen and nitrogen in order to avoid narcosis, but it means they have to stay in the water to decompress for up to five hours.

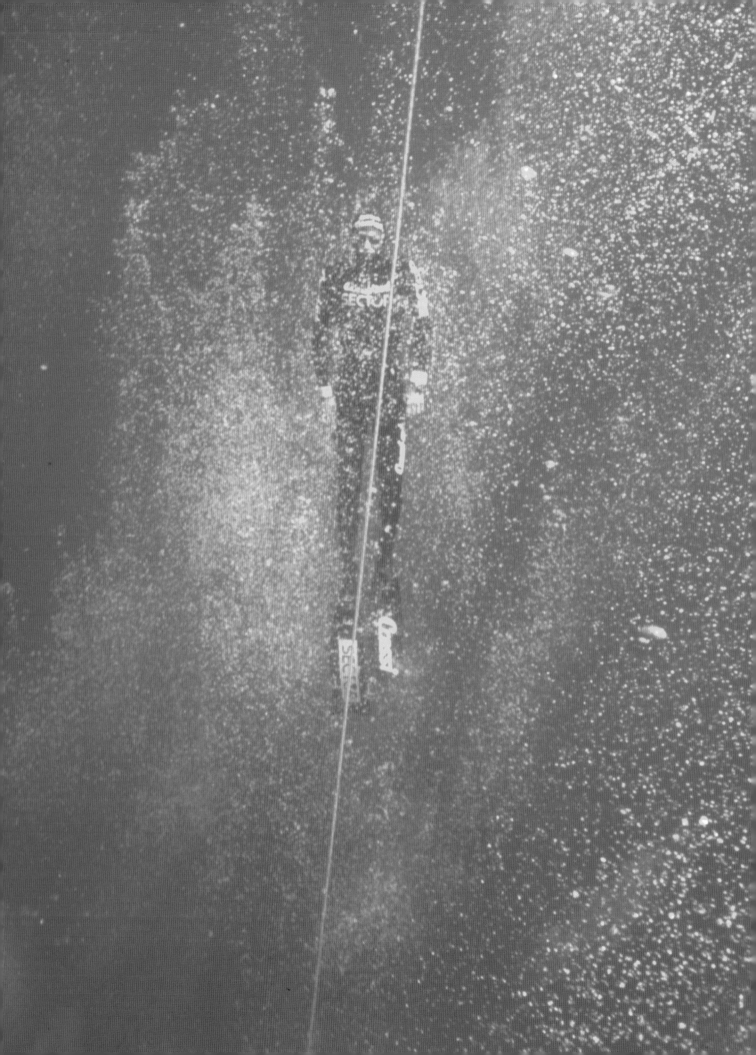

had built 'Precontinent II,' a small village 10 meters under the sea that a handful of men had inhabited for several days. The aim of the project, which was later expanded with Pre-continent III, was to determine how long a human being could live underwater, and to find out what physiological and psychological problems were entailed. The vestiges of that project were left on the bottom of the sea at Sha'ab er-Rumi: metal cylinders that resemble space-ships, and which Cousteau's men had installed on the sea floor in order to conduct their scientific experiments. Those rusty struc-tures, abandoned now for more than forty years, have both the appearance and signifi-cance of equipment left forever on a planet that has been discovered and explored and is thus no longer alien. It was here that Cousteau and his colleagues experimented for the first

time with the cages used for close encounters with sharks, and if today we divers can swim without fear amongst these magnificent crea-tures we owe it in part to their work.

I dove amongst them every day, watching them at close range. One day I was swimming with some white-tip and black-tip reef sharks (so called because their pectoral and dorsal fins are coloured white and jet black respectively) when we were joined by a large oceanic white-tip (*Carcharhinus longimanus*), easily recog-nisable by its enormous pectoral fins. It is a species that normally lives in deep water, but when it comes in to the shore it can become dangerous. The other sharks, who inhabit the reef and are generally non-agressive, changed their behaviour slightly, moving more freneti-cally and becoming generally more agitated. For the resident sharks the intrusion can bring

The explosion of joy upon surfacing with the record, the first after a depressing period of inactivity.

(on the previous page) A photo of the ascent from the 72 meter Constant Weight record dive. The descent line is like an umbilical cord that directs me towards the surface.

The breathe-up before my Variable Weight record dive to 105 meters – the most difficult moment of the whole attempt. Tension is running high. In my mind I revisit the hard months of training and sacrifices in order to confront my dive in the best condition possible. I cannot go wrong.

a danger of being attacked, or having to deal with a formidable competitor in the food chain.

Sharks are amongst the oldest vertebrates, and date back to some four million years ago. They have evolved very little, but in nature the term 'primitive' is if anything the opposite of derogatory. Their attributes make them unique in the animal kingdom: their skeleton is made up of cartilage instead of bone, and they have surprisingly stiff fins and tough skin made up of thousands of tiny scales arranged so that they confer exceptional hydrodynamic properties. The mako shark, which grows to four meters in length, can swim at speeds up to thirty-two kilometers per hour, which is an incredible speed to be moving through liquid. Another oddity of sharks is their enormous

liver, which can weigh up to 15% of the total weight of the animal. Being rich in Vitamin A, it allows the shark to keep a very slow metabolism, meaning it can go days without eating. Their great dimensions and high fat content allow the shark to float even though it doesn't have a swim bladder like almost all other fish.

The skin around the eyes and nose is full of special sensory organs called the Ampullae of Lorenzini, a series of small cavities filled with gelatinous liquid that holds the nerve endings which allow the animal to perceive the faintest magnetic fields conducted through the water. This can be used by the shark, for example, to detect the electrical signal generated by the heart beat of a flounder on the sea floor. This incredible sensitivity explains several behaviours that

I witnessed: during a night dive, while I was filming using a strong battery-powered lamp, a shark suddenly came at me with quick flicks of its tail – it was probably disturbed by the presence of the magnetic field generated by the batteries.

I was diving in the Red Sea every day, for days on end, amongst the grey sharks. I worked for a while as a dive guide, taking groups underwater and performing shark feeding sessions, which was a thrilling spectacle for the tourists. One day I was leading a group of Japanese divers who I had already taken diving on other occasions. I took them into the entrance of a large underwater cave, then brought down the food that we used to attract the grey sharks and lemon sharks (*Negaprion acutidens*). It was the jacks who arrived first

The jubilant surfacing after the dive, with all the safety divers that are descending on me to celebrate. These moments of immense joy and euphoria justify the countless hours spent training in the sea.

The true meaning of
freediving is not just
in the endeavour to
break records, but
in the sensations
that it gives you:
descending alongside
a sheer drop-off in
the most complete
silence; arriving on
the bottom and
stopping a moment
to watch the sun
rays filtering through
branches of coral…
I must not combat
the sea, instead every
component of my
being must become at
one with the water.

though, and although they are all small in size there was a large number of them. They swarmed around the burlap sack full of fish pieces, grabbing it and shaking it so that most of the contents spilled out. At this point the reef sharks, who I relied on for the show, descended together on the unsuspecting dinner party and began disputing the food in furious combat. I kept watching for a while, knowing that there was nothing I could do to stop the frenzy by that point, then turned to check on my Japanese clients to find that where I had left them at the entrance to the cave there wasn't a living soul. Could they have returned to the surface? I glanced upwards, but could only make out the silhouette of the hull of our boat. I started swimming into the cave, but when I found it empty I began to get seriously worried… Suddenly I heard a metallic sound, like a scuba tank hitting against rock, and looking into the blackness from where it seemed the sound came I saw my group of

Japanese attached to the ceiling of the cave like a colony of bats! Terrorised by the sharks' feeding frenzy they had inflated their buoyancy control jackets and been pushed up against the impassable rock of the cave ceiling, and now their position prevented them from lifting the purge valve above their heads so that they could deflate their jackets and descend down from that trap. On seeing such a comic scene I couldn't help but burst out laughing, and for a while I had difficulty even breathing through my regulator!

That same year, after spending the summer in the Red Sea, I went directly to the Maldives to begin my training. There, in the vastness of the open ocean, I concentrated on horizontal swims underwater: diving down to a certain depth and gliding along for a while before returning back to the surface. I would dive again and again, towing behind myself a dive float for safety which was attached to my weightbelt by a fifty meter long cord.

One time, as I was resurfacing I realised that something was preventing me from coming back up: something was holding me back with a soft, but nevertheless incontestable force. I assumed that the cord had wrapped itself around some coral, probably stag horn coral, which has numerous long branches like a leafless tree. I would never come back up from a dive on the limit of my breath hold, so I still had time to turn in the direction I had swum from to have a look and see what there was to be done. When I saw what was holding me under my heart leapt into my throat: an enormous fifteen meter long whale shark (*Rhiniodon typus*), black and covered in white spots.

The cord on my dive float had passed underneath its belly when that gentle giant had crossed silently and undetected above me. Calmly, and trying not to scare that beautiful animal, I released my weightbelt, which remained suspended on the cord held by the

(above)
I am 'flying' alongside a manta ray – a dreamlike creature. In its company I have experienced unforgettable dives.

float, then I pulled it back up and put it on again, and spent the next hour in the company of the whale shark, dancing with her to the tune of an inner music, feeling completely free alongside her in the blue of the ocean.

In the seas of the Maldives I was lucky enough to have many such exciting encounters. On another occasion I was able to swim with manta rays (*Manta birostris*). First cousins to the whale sharks, these harmless giants live in areas where the currents carry an abundance of their food source, plankton, and their huge mouths are flanked with two protuberances that serve to channel the food inwards. With a wingspan of up to four meters these huge rays use almost imperceptible movements to fly gracefully through the water: gliding, nose-diving, stalling, and performing loops like aerobatic pilots: all in order to swallow as much as possible of the tiny creatures that make up their diet.

Kids and dolphins

After the productive training in Sudan and the Maldives, I returned to Europe in the summer of 1996 for a new project that would also be beneficial to the Apnea Academy. In Spain I started holding courses for children: I wanted to see how they responded to apnea, how they were able to move underwater, and what they were interested in and attracted to. I noticed straight away that there was no sense in trying to explain the theoretical concepts, but rather it was better to get them first to enjoy themselves in the water, in such a way that through playing they could automatically and unconsciously acquire the techniques. They needed a little more time compared to an adult, but in the end they became fully aquatic. There has been medical research into the effect of apnea on children, and no negative impact or contraindications have been established. Of course a child should never be aiming for great depths, but rather a good mastery of the skills and safety awareness, and to this end we used a completely recreational approach to the swimming pool, recreating in that closed space of water a complete marine environment with seaweed and plastic fish. We invented challenges for the kids in a couple of meters of water. They were wearing wetsuits, but without weight belts, and this made everything more complicated: the wetsuit buoyed them up to the surface, and they would move clumsily and awkwardly to try and get down, without knowing why they were unable. They played and enjoyed themselves despite the handicap of the wetsuit's flotation. When I took them to the sea they were able to take off the wetsuits and suddenly they found themselves unencumbered and agile in the water with just their swimming costumes on. I had them wearing masks but with no snorkel, and for a particular reason. For many it was the first time that

they had seen the sea underwater: I would break sea urchins open in order to attract the little fish who would come to feed on the shellfish, or I would find an octopus and point it out to the children so that they could watch it move. It was an incredible discovery for them, and they would watch with their heads underwater for as long as they could hold their breath, then they would lift their heads out of the water and breath quickly two or three times before returning to apnea. They didn't want to 'turn off the TV' in order to breathe, and so they would stay tuned in, for as long as they could hold their breath, to that spectacle of live underwater action. Their curiosity and the pleasure of discovery got the better of their physiological drive to breathe, and they stayed in apnea without even realising it – this was the natural approach that I was aiming for.

On the last day of the course I took the kids to a naturally formed but closed-off inlet where

Freediving is peace and freedom. The dolphin, an animal considered sacred in many ancient cultures, symbolises these ideals more than any other sea creature. I've always closely observed the movements of this fascinating animal, and tried to imitate them. Even dolphins have to return to the surface to breath, and they are the best instructors on how to move underwater.

Crucial moments putting on my wetsuit before entering the water. Even here I am trying to maintain maximum calm and concentration. I try and create space around me. With my mind I am already in the sea.

a dolphin was living in captivity. There were about a dozen children, all of them excited, if a little apprehensive, and something incredibly beautiful happened. Amongst my students there was a deaf-mute little boy, and the dolphin, without hesitating, swam quickly straight towards him. The dolphin chose him. It seemed like the dolphin and the boy understood each other implicitly, and that the boy was able to communicate with the dolphin without difficulty. The rest of us felt excluded, as if in all the world there were only those two. They would take off swimming together and return together towards us, and when they looked each other in the eyes it was as if they understood one another. I had the sensation that the boy was so at home with the dolphin because in the soundless world into which he was born and continued to live he had become accustomed to communicating differently, with a silent language of gestures. Underwater, where it is im-

possible to say anything intelligible, he found a more hospitable environment – the opposite condition to his companions, who were a little unsettled by the silence of immersion and the necessity to communicate with signals. It was incredible that the dolphin was able to understand his situation, and put aside its incredible powers of communicating with sound. Because underwater isn't really 'a silent world,' even if that was the title of the first of Jacques Cousteau's famous documentary films. The density of water means that sound travels four times faster underwater than through air, and many sea creatures take advantage of this property of the liquid in which they live: some fish make loud noises to discourage potential predators, to attract attention or to locate prey. Cetaceans do it even more: male whales sing during mating season, dolphins communicate even at great distance with clicks and whistles, and the Amazon River Dolphin relies almost completely on

the auditory sense – it has small rudimentary eyes that do little good in the muddy river water. Using a kind of internal sonar the sperm whale is able to locate the squid it feeds on at a thousand or even two thousand meters, a depth where darkness reigns absolute.

After this experience I did a bit of research and discovered that studies had been done on 'dolphin therapy,' with autistic children placed in the company of cetaceans. In the space of very little time these children would enter into contact with reality, and start to manifest emotions and sentiments, overcoming the essence of their handicap. It was episodes like this one that convinced me that dolphins are truly special creatures: they are able to establish contact with human beings in situations where even we have little success, and they are able to open doors which would otherwise remain forever closed.

As far as I am concerned I am completely against dolphinariums, and I could never work at such a place – it would be too sad for me. One need only consider that dolphins kept in captivity die on average at the age of twelve, while in the wild they live fifty years or more.

There is a project which I am interested in however: one day I would like to look at the possibility of enclosing a large area of the sea and letting dolphins live there freely, so that they can be put in contact with autistic children, or people with serious difficulties in communication that might benefit from the interaction. At

the same time I would like to do something to put a stop to the massacre of dolphins and other marine mammals, in particular whales, who are still hunted for their meat despite international moratoriums. Furthermore, cetaceans are seriously disturbed by the sonar used by army vessels and fishing boats, which interfere with their organs of echolocation, impeding both their communication and their ability to hunt prey and thereby feed. Often certain species, especially pilot whales and Risso's dolphins, become stranded in large groups, and this is most often due to disturbances to their ability to echolocate. In other instances it is because one of the group who is hurt, weak, or ostracized, is cast by the waves on to the coast, and its cries attract the rest of the pod, who suffer the same fate.

An even greater menace is the threat of industrial fishing, which kills thousands of marine mammals every year, entangled in the mesh of trawlers or tuna nets. And when they aren't killed they are instead captured and imprisoned in every type of aquarium, dolphinarium or attraction park, trained to perform tricks and acrobatics. The conditions in which they are kept are sometimes good, sometimes deplorable, but in either case the dolphins still lose their freedom, their natural gaiety and most often their lives.

After this special mini-course I returned to Italy, just in time to wash my clothes before I left again for Croatia with my friend Ferdinand to return to my training program. It was the year 1996, and the nation had just ended its war of independence with the Republic of Yugoslavia. I discovered a breath-taking country, with practically virgin coastlines and waters. We were us-

(above)
I'm in a boat heading out to go spearfishing with Marco and Francesco.
The loss of Francesco was devastating, but with the help of Massimo (in the photo below on the left) I was able to overcome this difficult period. I dedicated both of my records of 1996 to Francesco.

ing a reinforced inflatable big enough to sleep in, and this allowed us to 'camp out' in any little bay or on any beach, and to reach the houses of fishermen who would from time to time take us in for a night – we made friends with almost everyone we met. We lived like this for about a month, and I would train every day as well as spearfish in order to provide food to eat. I returned around mid-August and began preparations to travel to Elba where my coach and team were waiting to begin the final stage of my training for the next world record attempts. On the 15th of August I called Massimo to tell him I was on my way, but from the tone of his voice I knew straight away that something was wrong. "I don't know how to tell you, but I have to: Francesco is dead. I found out yesterday. They called me from Greece, where he was spearfishing." It was tragic news. Francesco Boni was one of my closest friends and I had shared almost all of my spearfishing trips with him and Tore, a man from Santa Teresa di Gallura. When you dive all the time with a certain person, and you both look out for one another,

watching over each other while one is underwater and entrusting your lives to each other, there is an intimate and powerful bond that is formed between you. It is a link that might not exist in other situations, even with the closest of friends,. I couldn't think of anything other than Francesco, the spearfishing trips we had been on together, our rivalries, and the pranks we had played on each other during our conscript days. I couldn't take my mind off it.

At Francesco's funeral Massimo saw that I was badly shaken up. He asked me if I felt like concentrating on preparation for the records, perhaps dedicating them to Francesco. I told him I thought it was a good idea – it seemed like the only way I could honour the memory of a friend like Francesco, lost tragically while practicing the sport that was the foundation of our friendship. So we left for Sardinia.

In Villasimius the *Anfitrite* was waiting for us, and it would be our logistical base as it had been the year before. For support and transport from land to the *Anfitrite* we could still count on *Fiore di maggio*, owned by the charismatic fisherman Battista. I didn't know it yet, but 1996 would be my year of bad luck in terms of weather. Already in 1993 I'd had a taste of it, with my 123 meter record being delayed by several days, but from 1996 onwards I was never again given calm seas on the day of a record attempt. The *Anfitrite* had taken four times the normal amount of time to cross the stretch of the Mediterranean Sea between Palermo, Sicily and Cagliari in Sardinia, due to the heavy opposing wind and seas.

Nevertheless on the 9th of September we were able to attempt a Variable Weight dive to 110 meters: everything went well, and I broke Gianluca Genoni's 106m record. A week later, on the 16th I took the mark in No Limits to 131m, breaking Pipin's 128m record. I dedicated both of these world records to Francesco.

In Villasimius we had a new entrant to the team: 'Little David' Carrera, a super-passionate freediver who would become one of the top freedivers in the world, with an incredibly elegant style and aquaticity. From that moment on he became my trusted surface assistant, substituting Gianluca Genoni, who had started his own competitive career, and had a support team

The Pelizzari tribe, lined up for a family portrait. How I wound up being a freediver no one is able to explain: my mother is terrified of the water, and my father swims like a rock!

(on the next page) During the descent I enjoy the sensations that gradually seep into my body. I lose sensation in my legs, arms and torso. The only thing left is my head. I don't ever want to wake up from this dream.

of his own. If it's true that the hardest won victories are also the most memorable then I must say that the 131 meter dive that ended my season of 1996 is still very vivid in my mind. I still remember the late-night training sessions, which began at dusk when the wind and waves died with the sun, the numerous training dives that had to be cancelled due to impossible seas, and reckless dives in the most extreme conditions. At the end of the day the pair of records I set that year, and all the effort and stress that it took to get them, were excellent preparation for the record attempts to come, which were never again blessed by calm seas.

After celebrating the new records we returned to Elba, and there we decided to hold the first Apnea Academy Instructors course. The base would be a dive center owned by Alfredo Guglielmi, the Pirate, in Pareti di Capoliveri. There were about forty participants who wanted to improve their skills and learn the modern techniques. It was a legendary course, creating a group of new instructors ready to 'spread the word,' and who would become some of my closest friends.

As soon as the course had finished I transferred to Nice, where in November of that year the first freediving world team championships were being held, with eight nations competing. Each of the five athletes in a team had to compete in both Constant Weight and static apnea. The Italian team, which I was captaining, was made up of young up-and-comers, with a lot of natural talent and keen to perform well on their international debut. The competition started with static apnea, and the French – considered favourites because they were the home team and because they had been preparing for this event for some time – were ahead until the second to last diver. However the team must have had some kind of individual rivalry between its members which would cost them dearly: the fifth French athlete to compete tried to surpass the best time of one of his team mates, and ended up blacking out. Competition rules meant that the athlete was disqualified and any points earned up until the moment of the black out were taken away, resulting in a severe drop in the rankings for his team. This left us Italians in the lead. It was clear that we would be

able to claim the title as first world champions without having to push ourselves, so I advised my team to stay calm and not overdo anything. I then announced their Constant Weight attempts with depths well below their personal bests. It was the right move, as the end of the competition saw Italy in first place, followed by the French, with Colombia taking bronze.

This first edition of the world championships, even though it was attended by just a few nations, showed that something was moving in the world of freediving. The sport was no longer defined solely by the depth records of a select group of super-champions, and was becoming 'democratised' for a larger base of young freedivers, who were given the opportunity to test themselves against others and themselves in the first official contests. The victory of the Italian team in the first teams world championships confirmed the high standard within my country, and reopened a rivalry with the French that had long been established in all the other underwater sports.

A dolphin's smile

At the end of the year I left again for the Bahamas, to explore places that I had discovered on my previous voyage. I had to begin training again for the goals I had set myself in 1997, and I preferred to do it in warm waters. My first stop was Freeport on Grand Bahama, from where it is possible to reach deep water swimming off the beach, eliminating the need for a support boat. Training was going very well, and after a few weeks I decided to board a yacht as a member of its crew. One day we headed south, seven or eight hours from Freeport, to the Grand Bahama Bank, a huge expanse of shallow water with nothing but sand on the sea floor. It extends southeast of Miami and crosses the Northwest Providence Channel to form a wide curve about five hundred kilometers long between Cuba and the island of Andros. The edge of the bank is a clean line where the sandy flats drop off vertically into the abyss of the ocean, over two thousand meters below. A group of dolphins, mostly Atlantic Spotted dolphins and a few Bottlenose, have made this

their permanent home. We arrived on the bank close to Sandy Caye, a small tongue of dry sand, and the only piece of land visible above the water. We had been zigzagging along with the motors running at minimum for less than half an hour when a handful of dolphins appeared from out of the blue, looking keen to play in the trails of bubbles left by the boat's spinning propellers. We turned the motors off and jumped in to play with these completely wild and free-spirited dolphins. Within the pod there were a few females with their calves (baby dolphins), and it seemed like the mothers would encourage their offspring to come close to us and gain confidence. Every so often the group would move away in order to hunt, and then having completed their mission they would return back to us.

Amongst the guests on the boat there was a little five or six year old boy who didn't want to ever get out of the water. After several hours of swimming with the dolphins his parents ordered him to come back aboard, and I saw him afterwards in a corner of the deck, trying to hold back his hiccupping, but unable to stop a flow of tears. I tried to distract him, "Why are you crying?" I asked.

"Because I wanted to stay with the dolphins. The dolphins were smiling to me."

"They were smiling at you?"

"Of course, and do you know why?"

"No, please tell me!"

"Because when God created the Earth and all the creatures, he created the seas too, and put creatures in it: fish and sea mammals. Then he made a big palette to colour all the little fish and he made all the big fish blue and silver. But when it was the dolphin's turn God realised that he had finished up all his colours. So he said, "I want to make up for it. The dolphin won't be colourful but he will be the only creature in the sea who can smile.""

In the summer of 1997, as always I returned to the Mediterranean. I spent some time in Sardinia, but my logistical base was still on Elba, and I made the most of an incredible summer to prepare for new record attempts that were planned for the waters of Porto Venere in the region of Liguria. The organisation was formidable: the *Anfitrite*, loaded with technology and experience, was anchored permanently off the coast. The navy had loaned us land-sea craft in order to ferry myself and the numerous members who made up the complex machine of our team backwards and forwards between the land and the ship.

On the 13th of September I set a new world record in Constant Weight: 75 meters, two deeper than Alejandro Ravelo who had beaten my 72 meter record by a meter only a month earlier. Alejandro was new to the scene, and confirmed the strength of the Cuban freedivers.

That year I had another new team member called Roberto Chiozzotto, who was the second safety freediver after Davidino: one of the two would stay on the surface while the other would dive to meet me at 30 meters and accompany me from that depth until I took my first breath of air on the surface. This was a job that couldn't be designated to the safety scuba divers, who were required to stop their ascent close to the surface in order to decompress for a certain period. A week later, on the 20th of September, I took back the Variable Weight record as well, with 115m. Alejandro Ravelo had broken this too with 111 meters, and his record was only 11 days old when I took it back. That September the summer seemed to finish very early: both of my dives were made in particularly poor weather conditions, with high seas and steady gale force winds, and if it wasn't for the navy and their amphibian vehicles, which allowed us to reach the *Anfitrite* eight miles off the coast in pretty much any conditions, I would have inevitably had to delay the attempts. There is nothing worse for the emotional and psychological state of a freediver than having to postpone a record attempt that has been meticulously prepared for. When we celebrated my victory in the town square that evening I noticed that Tommasino Muntoni and the other Sardinian men in my team were all keeping a little to themselves, away from the rest of the group. They were obviously happy for me, but something was anguishing them, and although I noticed at the time there was too much else going on for me to find out what it was. It wasn't until the next day that I found

out the reason for their behaviour: in order to stop me from losing my focus before the attempt, and then afterwards to not ruin the celebration they had kept from me some terrible news, which had come to them at the moment that I was preparing to enter the water: Tore, my other companion from innumerable spearfishing trips, had been lost. The accident had happened in similar circumstances to how Francesco Boni had lost his life: Tore was trying to flush a grouper out of its cave at a seamount called Secca del Diavolo, ('Devil's Rock') offshore from Capo Testa, the exact same day as my record. "Pelo!" he had called me a couple of days before on the phone, "I'm going to come up to Elba as well..." I was forced to talk him out of it, as there wasn't a single space available, either in a hotel or on a boat. "Don't worry about it," I reassured him, "In two or three days when the job's done I'll come straight to Sardinia and we'll go spearfishing..."

Instead I left the same day that I found out that Tore had not come back from his dive. I knew that it was going to be even more difficult than at the funeral of Francesco, as this time we had to retrieve Tore's body from the sea and restore dignity to his death. Offshore from Capo Testa we easily found his spear gun – I knew

Dolphins transmit joy and serenity in every movement, and every expression contains a smile. Another good reason to learn from our marine cousins.

all too well the routes he followed while he was hunting. But his body was gone, and wouldn't be found until a month and a half later, far away in the south towards Alghero, where it had probably been dragged by the returning currents which would have first carried it as far as the coasts of Spain or France.

In the footsteps of Mayol

To prepare for the competitive fixtures of 1998, like the previous years I had to spend the winter in warm seas. I felt like discovering new places, and so I chose the far east. I started with Vietnam, in the South Chinese Sea, which although it was murky and somewhat cold offered seascapes that were entirely new to me. I spent a few days there before moving on to

Jacques Mayol's tales greatly influenced my choices of travel destination. I often retraced his footprints, and to see the peoples and places he visited was almost like hearing his stories again.

(on the next page) The Philippine fisherman who lived with his family on Snake Island, holding on to his outrigger canoe made from the trunk of a tree. His children, who were always happy and smiling, looked out for their father on his deep dives and cleaned the fish he would bring back to the canoe. The sea was their school and their lives.

Thailand, where I dove for a while in the waters of the island Similan in front of Phuket, and in the Andaman Sea. While there I recalled Jacques' stories about the tribes of nomadic fishermen in the southern islands of the Philippines, the *badjaos*, last remaining gypsies of the sea, free men and poets. Jacques had spoken many times of this dignified population of seafarers and fishermen who lived on and under the sea. The *badjaos* are for the most part Muslim, and speak several different dialects. They spend almost their whole lives aboard boats or in villages held above the lagoon on poles, so

their entire existence was carried out in complete intimacy with the sea. Most of them would learn how to swim and dive underwater well before learning how to walk. The *badjaos* children, especially the boys, had no time to go to school: their school was the sea, and as teachers they had only their parents. "The greatest freedivers I have ever seen at work," Mayol had assured me.

I travelled through some of the Philippine islands, and started asking for information on the *badjaos*. As always I tried to identify with the place in which I was staying, and the culture and customs of the people who were my hosts: I wanted to dive with the Philippine fishermen. I soon discovered that technology had prevailed over tradition here also, and there were very few of the real *badjaos* left.

However thanks to the help of a Philippine friend I was able to meet a fisherman who wasn't a member of that ethnic group, but lived alone with his family on Snake Island, an island named after its abundant population of sea snakes. I learnt that all sea snake species in that area were armed with a powerful poison, and a single bite could kill a grown man. However first they would need to bite him, and the extent that they could open their mouths prevented them from biting a human limb, let alone one covered in the neoprene of a wetsuit. The Philippine fishermen told me the only part of the human body at risk of being bitten was the earlobe, but in reality it was more likely that one of these serpents trapped on board in a net would bite someone in the webbing between one finger and the other. In any case it was on this scrap of well guarded rock that I met my fisherman. His vessel was a dugout canoe similar to those used in Polynesia, and made from the trunk of a large tree. Accompanied by his children, he came towards us, a heavy-built man who must have been around fifty years old, but could have easily passed off for thirty. He welcomed us warmly, like all the sea folk I have encountered in my travels, and we followed him with our boat to the site he had chosen for our diving. The water was crystal clear. The fisherman prepared his colossal speargun, a weapon made of at least two meters of extremely heavy wood, and armed with

corresponding big elastic bands. Compared
with our lightweight carbon fibre spearguns it
was a veritable antique! To complete the picture he was wearing huge swimming shorts,
goggles made from wood, and in place of fins
he sported two round sheets of plywood, which
were tied at the centre to his feet, a little like
old snow shoes, and forced him to swim using
a frog kick. There was no way to equalise the
airspace inside the wooden goggles, since the
two hollowed out cones only covered his eyes,
leaving his nose unconnected. They said that
this problem could be solved to a certain extent
by making the goggles out of balsa, the lightest
and softest wood known, and porous enough
to allow air to pass slowly into the goggles as
the pressure increased. Other fishermen who
practiced the same trade would make more sophisticated goggles, equipped with small rubber
pumps that released their air into the goggles
as the pressure increased. But the goggles used
by my fisherman seemed like they were made
from bamboo, not balsa, and there was no rubber pump. "He'll get to two meters before the
pain turns him round," I thought to myself. Far
from it: with his prehistoric equipment he descended to 20 meters without equalising once!

These days it only takes a few hours in a
plane to travel back in time, and in this case I
had gone back a hundred years.

I followed him, not wanting to participate
in the fishing trip, but rather just to observe.
He shot a fish that would have weighed barely
three hundred grams (I had seen very few large
specimens in this area), and placed it in his
canoe. On the surface, he held on to the canoe for a few moments, making strange loud
noises with his mouth as he breathed, before
returning underwater. In this way he speared
five or six fish, until his sons, who were clean-
ing the fish quickly with a knife, told him that
there were enough. He stopped fishing and
ripped his head first to one side then to the
other, before jiggling his finger energetically
in each ear in order to get rid of all the water,
then he climbed back onto his canoe. After
filleting the fish he took a bulb of garlic and
offered a clove to everyone present – I quickly
made up an excuse. He didn't insist, and with
his sons he ate the fish raw, from time to time

taking a bite from a piece of garlic, as if it was a hunk of bread or a slice of lemon. I felt like I was reliving Mayol's stories about the *bad-jaos*. Those nomadic fishermen had schooled Jacques as to the miraculous powers of garlic on the respiratory tracts, and he feasted on it every day. I had even tried this bizarre diet myself, but had straight away been ostracized by my friends…

I took my leave of the solitary fisherman, presenting him with my mask and hyper-technological fins as gifts. He looked suspiciously at those pieces of equipment, then thanked me with a smile and reached out from inside his canoe to shake hands vigorously, amidst bursts of laughter from his children. I believe he probably stayed faithful to his paddle fins, his wooden goggles and to his world that was so far from mine, taking from the sea only what he needed to survive, and nothing more. Meeting that Philippine fisherman – whose name I am ashamed to say I can't remember! – was like travelling back in time to the age of the pioneers of diving, two generations prior to my own, when in Europe spearfishers had to improvise everything, and knew nothing about apnea techniques or equalisation, and the technology and equipment was completely primitive. However I'm convinced that amongst the populations who practice this type of spearfishing there must be hidden many potential freediving champions.

In 1998 it was Italy, or to be more precise, Sardinia's turn to host the second World Teams Freediving Championships. I was returning from Asia, and keen to get back in the water, but I could no longer count on Francesco or Tore for my training spearfishing trips. Of course there were other people I could go with, but it would never be the same, and I realised this as soon as I arrived back in Sardinia. Wherever I went I always kept a photo of the three of us together in our boat, on our way out to go spearfishing. By now that photo is the only material record of our friendship and camaraderie.

That year I chose not to attempt any world records, partly because of the Teams World Championships. The competition would be held in Santa Teresa di Gallura, in Sardinia,

and from the eight teams of 1997 the number of nations competing had swollen to thirty five. This was the first year that I decided to base myself in Santa Teresa, a beautiful village of fishermen where in the visits of the previous years I had made many good friends like Tommasino and Gianni, people who were fond of me and had accepted me into their community. So it was that I bought a house overlooking the beach, fulfilling a dream that I had kept in my top drawer for so many years: to be able to open the window in the morning and look out to the horizon, and to be able to step out of my front door and within a few minutes have the water rushing around my ankles. The first time I came to Sardinia was before my competitive career as a freediver, about ten years previously, when I used to go spearfishing in Corsica. I had been in Bonifacio (the southernmost point of Corsica), and decided to catch the ferry across to Santa Teresa to continue my spearfishing trip further south. The only free place I could find was on the first ferry, which left at five in the morning, so by six o'clock I was already in Santa Teresa, and since I couldn't get to my friend's house at that ungodly hour I decided to hang out in the port and wait for dawn. After having breakfast in the port I walked up to the highest part of the village, from where you can look out over the port and the Straits of Bonifacio. The sun was rising in a blaze of colours, heralding a beautiful day ahead. "Now this is somewhere where I can see myself coming to live," I remember thinking to myself. At the time I was blown away by the panorama, and the incredible striking beauty of the place, and I didn't imagine that I would actually follow through with the idea.

So ten years later in 1998, when the world championships were held in my new home, I was involved in the organisation of the event. Once again Italy was to win the title, ahead of France, and this time the team was made up of myself, Gianluca Genoni, Paolo Saccavini, Gaspare Battaglia and Andrea Badiello. The average level of the entrants had increased notably, and even the average static apnea times were greater than any of the times reached in Nice the year before.

Diving with the Philippine fisherman was like taking a trip back in time. Round wooden plates instead of fins, underpants instead of a wetsuit, wooden goggles cracked by the sun, and a long but weak hand-made speargun. This kit, however rudimentary, was enough for him to be able to supply enough fish to feed his family.

The prize giving ceremony was held in the piazza (town square) at the centre of Santa Teresa. At the conclusion of the Italian national anthem I stood up on stage and dedicated our victory to Tore. In front of his community, in front of the sea that had taken him away a year before, and in front of his tearful mother Giuseppina, the crowd erupted in a thunderous applause. Tore must surely have heard us.

No world records for me that year then. I decided instead to venture into a new and slightly different type of attempt, a kind of demonstration and commemoration at the same time. I'd had the idea the year before in Japan, during a presentation by my sponsor Sector Watches, which was launching its marketing campaign in that country. One evening I was at dinner with the president Filippo Giardiello, the Norwegian polar explorer Børge Ousland, the free climber 'Manolo' (Maurizio Zanolla) and the

famous French skydiver Patrick Gayardon, four members of the Sector 'No Limits' Team, a selection of athletes from extreme sports. Børge Ousland had just returned from a failed solo attempt to cross the Antarctic, and showed us all his photos. For an error that is unforgivable at his level he had forgotten to wear his leggings, and exposed to temperatures as low as -38°C the skin on the insides of his thighs had first chafed, then adhered to the material of his trousers, making terrible sores. De Gayardon could relate to this: "It's the same for me when I jump out of a plane at over ten thousand meters – it's as cold as hell, even -70°C… My mask turns into a block of ice, and I have to wear two diving wetsuits, with a third suit over the top that's very aerodynamic so I can get down quickly to where it's a bit warmer and there's more oxygen." In fact he told us that he was forced to make his jumps in one of the coldest places on the planet, Siberia, and during the

coldest time of the year, midwinter! This was to avoid great changes in temperature during the jump, which might put excessive stress on his heart. The president listened to him in rapture. Then it was Manolo's turn: "Yeah, I screwed up in the mountains once too. I was pitching a tent at base camp when a gale came through. I lost all sensation in my hands, so I took off one of my gloves in order to hold one of the pegs I was putting in the ground. I paid for it with two frozen fingers."

I sat there not knowing what to say, or what kind of story to tell. I carried on eating with my head kept low, but when I realised that my four companions were waiting for me to say something I finally lowered the collar of my shirt and said, "Look at this! I just got back from the Philippines, and I didn't have any sunscreen with me. Check out this sun burn!" Giardiello burst out laughing, saying, "This is a dinner for No Limits men – what kind of No Limits man are you? In your sport you're spoilt rotten: special wetsuits, contact lenses, carbon fibre fins… The real No Limits divers were those sponge fishermen from the start of the century who used to go to crazy depths with just a big old stone to pull them down: no mask, wetsuit or fins… That Greek guy, what was his name? The one that brought up the anchor from one of our navy boats?"

The president had often talked to me about this Greek sponge fisherman, Stathis Haggi, who retrieved the ship's anchor of the battleship *Regina Margherita*, in the Bay of Pegadia, on the island of Karpathos between Rhodes and Crete. The ship had been moving slowly into the bay when the captain decided to lay anchor, since the first mate who was trained to take depth soundings had told him the bottom was only 30 meters. In just a few moments everything went wrong: the chain ran out quickly, seemingly without touching any bottom, and the huge ring at the end of the chain was torn out of the chain pit by the backlash. Freeing itself from the windlass it struck the first mate (killing him on the spot) as well as several other seamen. This was a huge tragedy for the ship, beyond the loss of the anchor and chain. In their review of the accident they discovered that as the anchor was descending the forwards

I love diving in the open water, with hundreds of meters of sea below me. The blue has an added intensity, and the sun rays disappear into the abyss, where I go chasing them…

movement of the boat had brought it past the edge of a steep drop-off.

News of the disaster spread quickly, and when the ship returned to Karpathos after having unloaded the body of the officer in Rhodes, a man came forwards to offer his services. His name was Stathis Haggi, and he was a local sponge fisherman. Haggi said that he would be able to retrieve the anchor by passing a rope through the chain. In his work he claimed to have reached a depth of 110 meters, and to be able to stay at 30 meters for up to seven minutes without breathing.

The bottom where the anchor was lying had been surveyed, showing a steep slope from 65 to 85 meters. The friends who came along with the fisherman were sure that he was up to the task, and the captain was eventually convinced

to trust their judgement – after all it wouldn't cost anything to let him try, even if such a feat was considered blatantly impossible in those times.

Haggi's method was ingenious, and quite similar to that used for modern day records. Before each dive he would wash his mouth and nasal cavities with salt water, and breath forcedly (what is now called 'hyperventilation'). He

would descend with the use of a square, flat slab of slate that weighed fourteen and a half kilograms, attached to a line that was unspooled and then hauled up by two helpers in the boat. Haggi's left wrist was connected to the stone with a short lanyard containing a loop that the descent line ran through. On the way down he held the stone tightly in his hands, using it like a rudder to maintain a vertical descent, then he would place it on the bottom in order to work, leaving it there as a point of reference so that when he wanted to come back up he could give a quick tug on the line and hold on to the rock while his friends quickly hauled the line back in. From what is understood he had no need to equalise. He wore no mask, and had no fins on his feet: neither had been invented yet.

The depth at which the anchor lay must have been at least a little challenging for Haggi, since he spent the whole first day training to increase his operating depth. The following day he made a good five dives to the chain, and was able to attach a grappling hook to it at 84 meters. On the third day he dove seven times to the end ring at 77 meters, and was finally able to secure it with a wire cable. The day after a second rope was tied to the chain, which had been lifted several meters with the first rope: now it was up to the seamen on board the *Regina Margherita* to winch it in. Including the training dives the whole job was concluded in twenty one dives over four days, at depths between 45 – 84 meters.

The most astonished person of all was the ship's doctor, who wrote in his logbook: "Haggi came back up from each dive in full control, and demonstrated this by the way he would climb back on board his boat without help from his comrades and start clearing his nose and ears of the water that had entered them during the dive. Haggi asserted that he felt pressure on his shoulders but none in his ears. He also stated that at 80 meters the water is very clear, and there is still enough light to work with." The doctor was bewildered by Haggi's feat, which went against all the current theories of the time regarding the human body's capacity to withstand pressure. This happened in 1913, but even in 1960 the French doctor Cabarrou, medic for Jacques

(above)
Stathis Haggi in full
diving equipment:
a kind of kimono,
yellowed by the sun,
and a stone used to
carry him down.
He had a slender,
almost emaciated
physique, which
demonstrates that
all that matters for
freediving is will
power and mental
control.

Cousteau's dive team, declared that "the human limit is 50 meters, and beyond this depth the body will implode." The Italian doctor onboard the *Regina Margherita* proposed a theory whereby Stathis Haggi might be able to breathe subcutaneously from the air dissolved in water, and that this was aided by the pressure. This theory was supported by the fact that, during his medical exam, when the doctor asked him to hold his breath he only managed forty seconds(!) Regarding this exam, the doctor wrote in his logbook: "Even though my exam showed a significant pulmonary emphysema, the upper thorax does not exceed average proportions, and is convex and rigid. The heartbeat is faint

hold his breath in atmospheric conditions he reached forty seconds, while during his diving to recover the anchor he was underwater for periods between 1:30 and 3:35."

For my sponsor the exploits of this Greek sponge fishermen from other eighty years ago were the epitome of No Limits. So I told my tormentor, "OK, since that Greek fished up the anchor from 80 meters, I'll bet you that next year I can dive to 100 meters using only a stone, just like him…"

Giardiello accepted the wager immediately, and as soon as I got back to Sardinia I started preparations for this commemoratory dive. Naturally I thought it best to do the dive in the waters of Karpathos, where eighty five years earlier Stathis had brought back the *Regina's* anchor. It would also be an opportunity to make a comparison between the equipment of a modern-day freediver and that used by an ancient Greek sponge fishermen. At home

(on the next page)
My preparation in the
final minutes before
what would come to
be known as the most
beautiful performance
of my career. Carried
only by the weight of
a stone, and without
fins, mask or wetsuit
I dove to 100 meters,
using the technique
of the Greek sponge
fishermen.

but regular, and between eighty to ninety beats per minute, while breathing rhythm is twenty to twenty two breaths per minute. Auditory function is reduced, due to a complete lack of eardrum in one ear, and only partial eardrum in the other. When asked to

in Sardinia my training was thorough and intense – diving to 100 meters with only a stone to take you down is still a pretty difficult assignment.

In September, on Karpathos, everything was ready: a line measured out to 100 me-

ters, a stone carved into a seven kilo block, and a swimming costume. There were no officials, judges or crowds, but my whole team was present. At last I dove. It was a beautiful freedive: I felt like the sea was caressing me, that my body was at one with and enclosed by the water. I fell headlong into the abyss, trying to maintain the most hydrodynamic body position in order to maximise the thrilling sensation of speed… I was so concentrated that when I arrived at the bottom and the rope ran out with a jolt I almost lost my grip on the weight! I turned, grabbed the rope, and just like the sponge fishermen of a hundred years ago I returned to the surface with long pulls on the rope. I had surpassed my heroic predecessor by almost twenty meters, but most importantly I won the bet with the president of Sector! The dive, and all that it entailed constituted a tough undertaking: to freedive to 100 meters in a swimming costume, sustaining every several meters the icy shock of a thermocline – where the water temperature can drop suddenly by as much as three to five degrees Celsius – was a brutal ordeal for someone who is accustomed to diving with a wetsuit. The second problem was equalisation: when weighted down by a seven kilogram stone after a certain depth you reach a breakneck speed of descent, and I had to train specifically to be

A sequence of photos from the 'Greek freedive.' The weight of the rock that took me to the bottom caused a rapid acceleration of the freefall to close to four meters per second. The most difficult aspect of the dive was equalisation, as I had no means of being able to slow the descent. Without knowing it, in 1913 Stathis Haggi became the first record holder in the history of freediving. While I was trying to exceed his depths I discovered the enormous difficulties involved in a dive of this type.

I return to the surface, carrying with me the memory of unique sensations. My unprotected body was crushed by eleven kilograms of pressure on every square centimeter of skin. I felt like I was a speck in the ocean, and I was aware of the power of nature.

able to equalise quickly enough. In addition I had no brake, as I do on the sled, nor did I have fins that could be flared in order to create drag and slow the descent when I was having difficulty equalising. The only thing I would have been able to do was let go of the stone and call a support diver to take me back to the surface, since at those depths if you tried to come back swimming breaststroke you could kiss goodbye to the idea of seeing the sun again…

It was interesting to be able to experiment, as a modern freediver, with diving techniques that have by now been abandoned for quite some time. I also enjoyed talking with the oldest inhabitants of the island, who still remembered that legendary event, since the captain of the Regina Margherita had celebrated the recovery of the anchor with the whole community. In the town square they had organised a gigantic feast, and for the first time in their lives the islanders had tasted Italian spaghetti!

My life, the sea

MORE THAN ALONE, ON THE EDGE OF THE SEA
I ABANDON MYSELF LIKE A WAVE TO THE
CYCLICAL TRANSFORMATION OF THE
WATER IN WATER, AND OF THE ME IN ME

Paul Valéry

Stefania, a dolphin returned to the sea

I came back from Greece full of enthusiasm, and buzzing from a singular experience that gave me nothing in terms of sporting performance, but which enriched me as a freediver and as a man. The dive itself was very difficult, and everyone who knows me agrees that this tribute to the dives of Stathis Haggi was one of my most important achievements.

In the meantime there was a new project on the horizon, very different to the last, but just as symbolic. A French production company had contacted me regarding a television series on the sea. The hero would be a captive dolphin who would regain her freedom, and it was my task to accompany her on her return to the wild.

The dolphin was called Stefania, a female bottlenose who had been captive for twelve years in a circular pool about twelve meters across and a meter and a half deep, on San Andrés, a Caribbean island that is part of

Colombia, even if geographically it is a lot closer to Nicaragua.

The entire operation had been assigned to a hand-picked team: the veterinary doctors Cyril Hue and Olivier Van Canneyt from the centre for research on marine mammals in La Rochelle, the American Ric O'Barry (trainer of Flipper, the dolphin star of the television series of the same name that I had watched religiously as a kid), and myself. My job on San Andrés would be to spend as much time as possible in the water with the dolphin, observing her behaviour and dietary habits and giving reports to the vets and the trainer. O'Barry came from a background of conditioning wild dolphins who were captured and placed in the confined spaces of the dolphinarium, where they were trained to perform dances and tricks that justified the price of a ticket. However for several years he had been doing the opposite: taking dolphins who had spent long years in captivity and teaching them to fend for themselves once they were released back into their natural habitat.

I'm swimming with Stefania, a dolphin kept for many years in captivity. My role was to stay in the water with her as much as possible, and observe how she fed, but most importantly to keep her from feeling lonely during her adaptation to the new environment.

Stefania was to be placed in monitored freedom, under constant observation by the vets, and rehabilitated and trained while being documented for the television series, at the end of which the dolphin would be released finally into the wild ocean. It promised to be a fascinating job and a unique experience, and I was impatient to get going.

My journey began with the first stop in Bogota, then a flight for San Andrés where I met up with the other three members of the team. We immediately began talking about the initial idea: to transport the dolphin to Albuquerque, a small island about fifty miles away which had an area of the sea cordoned off where we could begin Stefania's return to freedom. However as soon as we arrived at the dolphinarium it was clear that before we could consider taking the poor cetacean back to the wild we would have to act without delay to save her life. Two other dolphins who had been kept in the same complex, Chico and Lady, were dead from an infection. Stefania was reduced to a terrifying con-

dition: she floated inert in her cement-walled pool, amidst dirty water, and refusing to eat. In two weeks she had lost sixty kilos, and the deformation of her head – which now looked like an enormous peanut – didn't leave us with much hope for her life.

Stefania was incapable of opening her mouth, her eyes were closed over by secretions from her tear ducts, her skin was being overrun by fungus and had been burnt by the sun because she was now incapable of keeping herself underwater. Of all these ailments the most dangerous condition to her life was dehydration. Like all marine animals that don't have access to fresh water, dolphins acquire this liquid that is indispensible to all forms of life on earth directly from their prey. So the biggest concern of her not eating was that it meant she was not drinking.

There was no time to lose. We started immediately by building a makeshift shelter that would protect Stefania from the potent tropical sun, but the unfortunate animal was still refus-

When she was put in the sea for the first time in her life Stefania experienced the effects of waves and currents, and she was unable to deal with it. She was pushed again and again onto the shore, beaching herself on the sand. In this phase I was the only reference point she could count on, and she often looked at me as if she wanted to ask for my help.

pool to hug the wretched animal, speak sweetly to it, and caress its afflicted skin. It was in that precise moment that the miracle recovery of the dolphin began.

Thanks to the constant presence of Veronica, Stefania began to open her eyes and swallow the mixtures of pureed fish and fresh water that were squirted into her mouth with a large syringe. After a while the fresh water was replaced with Gatorade, a sports drink rich in sugars, and finally they even mixed in medicines appropriate for her desperate condition. Little by little she began to recover, but she still didn't have the strength to float, and was placing her tail on the bottom of the pool in order to get her blowhole out of the water so that she could breath. The water was being changed often, but it was the same tiny pool, and although our task was still to save the dolphin and return her to freedom in the sea, she was still too sick to undertake the journey. So we had to wait for several weeks in order for Stefania to regain her strength.

Finally the big day arrived. With the help of men from the Colombian naval base on the island we managed to get the suffering dolphin onto a special stretcher and transfer her from the dolphinarium to a military truck, which in ten minutes brought her to the port. A boat was waiting for us there, the *Caracol*, with a ten centimeter deep pool for Stefania. Using a kind of toboggan, and as delicately as we could, we slid Stefania into the shallow pool. We had applied lanolin and hydrating cream to her skin, so she was completely white, and we could only make out her wide, anxious eyes that observed the turmoil around her. Veronica was with her in the water, using a sponge to keep her wet and pet her lovingly. It was going to be a long voyage, potentially fatal to a dolphin so weakened by sickness.

Finally, after seven or eight hours we reached Albuquerque, a small circular island about a hundred and fifty meters across, closer to Nicaragua than to Colombia. It was a natural paradise of white sand beaches, palm trees and mangroves, without either fresh water or electricity. The only inhabitants were four soldiers who worked shifts of two to three weeks. Ric O'Barry had chosen the island in order to

As the months passed I realised that Stefania had less and less need for me. It made me a little sad, but I knew it was right this way: in order to live completely free in her sea she would need to forget every tie with man.

ing any kind of treatment that Ric and Olivier tried to give her. At this point the manager of the 'concentration camp' where Stefania had been kept had the idea to call Veronica Duport, a Swiss girl who had looked after Stefania for five years, but who had walked out, saying that she wouldn't return until the day that the dolphin was set free. Two days later Veronica arrived on San Andrés. She was still holding her bags when she saw Stefania for the first time, and she started crying and hiccupping desperately, as she jumped, fully-clothed, into the

prevent the bay where we would keep Stefania from becoming a tourist attraction, with people wanting to come and swim with the dolphin. In the evening we used kerosene lamps for light, and all our fresh water was stored in large jerry cans – I felt a little like Robinson Crusoe!

On the southern coast the team had constructed an enclosure forty meters square in a lagoon protected by coral reef and descending gradually to a depth of 3 meters. We carefully lowered Stefania into her new home in the sea.

Echolocation is a sense used by dolphins that allows them to 'see' their surroundings by means of very high frequency sound waves, whose reflections (echoes) are sensed by the dolphin's ear, and interpreted by the brain, which uses the coordinates (size, distance, depth, form, internal composition) to create an 'image' of the object. A 'sixth sense,' or more accurately the maximum expression of the auditory sense, it is completely useless in a dolphinarium, where there is no necessity to hunt in order to eat since all food is provided by the keepers.

It was a beautiful scene: for the first time in twelve years the dolphin was in her element. Veronica had dreamt about this moment, and couldn't hold back her tears of joy. However it was immediately apparent that Stefania wasn't reacting as a dolphin would. She had become accustomed to hearing the ultrasonic waves of her echolocation bouncing off the walls of her tiny prison-like pool, and now since the ultrasounds she emitted didn't encounter any obstacle she couldn't understand where she was.

Furthermore Stefania was thrown off balance by the waves and current. With her muscles atrophied from twelve years of swimming circles in still water, she moved clumsily in the sea and constantly wound up on the beach. I was in the water with her for twelve hours straight: twelve hours of reassuring her and rescuing her from the beach where she would collapse in resignation, and bringing her back to the deep water so that she could learn to swim again. Her dorsal fin was curled over on her

Stefania, Ric O'Barry and I in the natural enclosure created in the waters of Albuquerque, where we conducted the phase of rehabilitation. At the end it was an enormous satisfaction to see Stefania living in the sea, when she had risked death in captivity only months ago.

back, just like the orcas who are also kept in the most famous of those concentration camps for cetaceans.

Ric decided to move on with her diet, and try to get Stefania to eat freshly killed sardines, instead of frozen ones. It might seem like an easy task, but in reality this was a disconcerting change for an animal who hadn't eaten anything but frozen sardines. It took two months and a lot of patience to get past this barrier before we started with the second phase, in which Stefania was given all forms of fish to eat. When she was released and we stopped feeding her she wouldn't be able to find many sardines in these waters. We had

Before entering the water for a freedive I try and attain a state of maximum concentration. Mayol often told me that the result of a deep dive is determined during the preceding breathing and relaxation on the surface.

to wait almost three months before the results were satisfactory – even in this second phase I was constantly in the water alongside Stefania, ready to reassure her, pet her and console her if I saw that something was stressing her. I realised that the dolphin was gradually becoming more autonomous, more independent, more herself. When I got in the water she still swam towards me to say hello, just like a big happy dog, and she still took food from my hands, but during the day she would more and more frequently go off by herself to explore her large enclosure. In the meantime we created a larger enclosure on the northern side of the island, where the water was 15 meters deep, and here Stefania would undergo the third phase of her return to freedom, in which she would learn to dive to greater depths and deal with the effects of the pressure, as well as learn to hunt for her own food. In order to do this she would have to forget the human beings who had fed her for her entire life. The two vets, Cyril and Olivier, as well as Veronica would no longer be allowed in the water with the dolphin. Ric would be with her to a limited extent in the first few days, while I would be the only one who would continue to swim at her side to observe her behaviour, but the moment in which I saw her start to catch her first fish then I would have to leave also.

Finally the day for the move came: Stefania was eating any type of fish that was given her, and we could conclude phase two and transfer her to the deep enclosure. While Cyril and Olivier examined her for the last time, Veronica lovingly petted her healed back. The dolphin was taken to her new deeper home where she would have to learn to feed herself. The moment she touched the water we witnessed the most beautiful thing: Stefania seemed to want to express her gratitude for having taken her from that tub of filthy water and restored her to the ocean: she swam off from us quickly, but immediately turned, and keeping her head out of the water she looked at each of one us individually in the eyes. When I entered the water to make sure she was alright Stefania was already at the opposite end of the enclosure, but she came swimming back again towards the beach and towards me, rubbing against my legs, biting my hands delicately and making tiny squeaks and clicks. Taking food from my hands she was like a big puppy, and when she peacefully swam off again after her encounter with her human friend her great horizontal tail was wagging with fluid undulations. In that moment I could relate to Veronica and her hiccups.

The mission wasn't finished however. We had to start catching fish with a fishing line and releasing them into the sea next to Stefania, hoping that she would take advantage of the temporary stunned state of her potential prey. Before putting them back in the sea Ric would cut the fishes' dorsal fins so that Stefania would be able to hunt them easier. Ric and I argued about the reasoning behind this, as he was completely against spearfishing and didn't hesitate to tell me why, but I attested that no one gave us the right to make fish suffer in order to save a dolphin. However the first trials weren't successful – the fish escaped, swimming raggedly away before the dolphin could bite them. After a while though Stefania started to get hungry, and since we weren't providing her with food any more it was up to her to get it for herself. When she chased and caught the first live prey in her entire existence she celebrated the moment with a huge jump out of the water. In the days that followed Stefania became more and more adept at catching her own fish, even those that hadn't been hooked and released. Ric and I watched her discretely, at an increasing distance, in order to ensure that everything was going well. We began gradually thinning out our time in the water. One night a violent storm dragged away the poles that held the netted walls of the enclosure, and the morning after when we discovered the damage we noticed that Stefania hadn't taken advantage of the circumstances, and had remained inside the space she knew and trusted, not daring to venture beyond what were now only virtual borders.

We spent a week like this, not knowing exactly what to do, before Ric had an insight: our dolphin wasn't drawn to the open sea because in that area there were no pods

of her species who could take her in. We couldn't expect that a dolphin who had lived in captivity her whole life, even if she had now learnt how to find her own food, could survive without having been adopted into a pod of other wild bottlenose dolphins who could teach her how to navigate and make do in open water. Stefania had to be transferred somewhere else.

We organised a special convoy, and after an interminable voyage we brought Stefania to the Caribbean waters of the island of Rosario, in front of Cartagena in Northern Colombia. Here there was a kind of natural dolphinarium, a semi-closed inlet where many groups of bottlenose dolphins were living. We freed Stefania, who started swimming away with great leaps, but we didn't abandon her completely. While humans can be told apart by their fingerprints, the same applies for the dolphin's dorsal fin, which varies in size, shape and angle. Many months later we recognised Stefania's fin right amongst a pod of her species, and shortly after she was pregnant, then she had her own young...

The mission was accomplished. A dolphin who several months previously was dying in a tub of dirty water was now living in the wild. We had restored an incredible animal to its natural environment, in the big blue. Afterwards we didn't look for Stefania any more.

We don't freedive to look around, but to look inside. During a dive with scuba tanks you can take photos to show what you've seen to your friends, but what you see and feel during a freedive can't be expressed in an image.

(on the next page) The Constant Weight descent. Without any external help, it is the most pure and technical of the disciplines. If you dive deeper than another athlete then you are the better freediver.

On board the *Anteo*, moments before entering the water for an attempt at the Constant Weight world record.

Portofino 1999: the 150 meter mark falls

I began to think about closing my career with world records, if possible in style. I wanted to dedicate my time to other things, especially after this incredible experience with 'Estefania,' as the Colombians had christened our dolphin in Spanish.

I first talked about it with Massimo Giudicelli. The end of our great escapades in deep freediving would be heart-breaking for him, but obviously in this case the decision could only be my own. In any case, before I made any final decision I had to finish the program we had established for 1999.

I knew I could count on a first-class organisation and logistical base on board the navy boat *Anteo*, a craft designed to provide multipurpose underwater assistance in emergencies. The ship was equipped with laboratories, a decompression chamber and a hyperbaric therapy center for dives with helium-oxygen mixes. It even had a small submarine, a rigid diving suit that could operate to 350 meters for three hours and a bathysphere that could go to 600 meters. Most importantly the *Anteo* was the boat used by the legendary technical divers and operatives of the Italian navy. I had long worried about the fact that, while my safety divers were there to intervene in the event of an emergency with a freediver, no one could help the divers themselves if one of their number had a problem at depth. *Anteo* was the solution to this important problem, and provided both myself and my team with the greatest level of safety.

I returned home to Sardinia and resumed my training. At the end of August I left for Elba, to begin preparing with Massimo for what should have been my last season as a competitive freediver. The date was set for around mid-October, and the venue was in the waters of Portofino in Liguria, north-west Italy. Since it was my last opportunity I wanted to set world records in all three disciplines: Constant Weight, Variable Weight and No Limits.

I decided on 80 meters for Constant Weight, given that in Syracuse the previous year Alejandro Ravelo had taken the record for the discipline to 76 meters. He had beaten my 75 meter record by a single meter, and in pretty suspicious circumstances: by all accounts he had come to the surface unconscious, but the dive had somehow been ratified by CMAS. I wanted to regain my record, and decisively too, given that it was taken from me so dubiously. Also in 1998, Gianluca Genoni had added two meters to Pipin's No Limits record, diving to 135 meters at Porto Ottiolu. In June of 1999 Loïc Leferme, a young and talented French diver, had beaten this, setting his first world record in No Limits with 137 meters, but it had been quickly taken back by Genoni with 138 meters, again at Porto Ottiolu. So at that time my objectives were to beat Ravelo's 76 meters in Constant Weight, and Gianluca Genoni's 122

The wall of 80 meters is broken in Constant Weight. I have just set a record and beaten another athlete, but I haven't beaten the sea. I will never defeat the sea – instead it is the sea that allows me to win.

meters in Variable Weight and 138 meters in No Limits.

The *Anteo* was equipped and ready, and I was introduced to the captain, his first mate and the team of divers, all of them enthused by a great passion for deep diving. We had new members to the team: Gigi Poli and Jorge Rodas, a great Colombian freediver who I had met in Nice in 1996, and who I had stayed in contact with, building a close friendship. Gigi was in charge of organisation outside of the team, a delicate task given that the depths for the safety divers were becoming so serious, and the support of the *Anteo* allowed us to provide assistance to the divers during decompression. As the depths increased everything was becoming more complex.

The first attempt would be 80 meters in Constant Weight. The sea had been smooth and calm during my training in Sardinia, and September in Elba, although it had given a couple of signs of inquietude. On Monday the 18th of October I habitually donned my wetsuit, entered the water and began my breathe-up. I started visualising the entire dive as I would have to perform it: the duck dive that would begin it all, the equalisation I would need to effect, the strong finstrokes at the start of the dive becoming lighter as I approached

the freefall, which would take me inexorably towards the plastic tag at the end of the taut descent line. I saw myself at the moment I would take the tag, without force, and hold it carefully in my fist: that piece of white plastic is the testimony of depth – the whole reason for my dive. This virtual dive was an indispensable part of my preparation. Afterwards I stretched out, breathed deeply, and when I felt ready I gave the five-minute signal. Every member of my team assumed the position he had been assigned.

The countdown reaches zero. I take one last deep breath, immerse my head, move my fins a couple of times to push me forwards through the water, then lift my legs to use their weight to sink my body under the water. When my fin blades are fully submerged I begin finning forcefully. My eyes are closed, but I open them every five meters or so to make sure I am travelling vertically next to the seemingly endless descent line. At 40 meters I stop finning, and continue in freefall towards the plate at 80, trying to maintain the most hydrodynamic shape possible. The palms of my outstretched hands work like little rudders, with small movements to correct my trajectory. Now I'm at the bottom, and I widen my eyes and let myself fall towards the tag that denotes the target depth. I seize it, tear it from the plate and grip it tight in my fist. Now begins the hardest and most dangerous part of the dive, the phase of suffering: the ascent. I have to fill my mind with positive thoughts, and maintain a fluid and rapid finstroke. I close my eyes again so that I can concentrate better on myself and so that the meters might pass more quickly. When I reach a depth of 40 meters I have to tell myself that I am *already* halfway there – I can't let myself think that I *still* have halfway to go. My legs feel like heavy wood, but my mind steps in to say, 'everything's going fine – my legs are fresh, there's no problem.'

I continued upwards, and the moment my face finally broke the surface I felt an extraordinary, intense joy. Alejandro Ravelo's record had been broken, and with it a boundary that had been considered by many to be insurmountable in this most athletic and challenging of the freediving disciplines, Constant Weight. I was totally satisfied, especially because I had been able to keep the promise I'd made to my fans the year before: a new world record, with an increase of four meters. I was very happy with how my training had gone, especially the techniques of concentration and relaxation. During preparation with Massimo I had completed training dives to depths of 81 – 82 meters. He believed that I should reach the target depth ten to fifteen days before the attempt date, and then spend the remaining period working at that depth. This is very important, since the day of the attempt everything changes: psychologically it's difficult to recreate the calm and peaceful atmosphere of a training dive alone with your team in the sea. So it is a huge help if you're able to tell yourself that what you're trying to do you've already done ten times before in training.

We didn't have time to celebrate however, as I had to start thinking about a Variable Weight attempt in order to beat Genoni's 122 meter record. We had planned a training dive to 120 meters on Tuesday the 19th, followed by 125 meters on Wednesday. Everything proceeded as planned until Thursday, when a particularly violent storm blew over, whipping the seas into a frenzy. The coast guard sent out a warning, and the *Anteo*, anchored seven miles off from

Portofino, received orders to return to port in Genoa. Captain Renda called us up and said, "We've seen the forecast and there are another four storms like this one all lined up in a queue. I think you might be best off just concentrating on one of the two disciplines, Variable Weight and No Limits, and try and squeeze in an attempt between one storm and the next."

Everything was conditional however. In order to attempt anything the *Anteo* would have to leave port and anchor at the dive site, and this operation alone required three quarters of the day. After the telephone call Massimo called a team meeting to decide how to go ahead, considering the captain's advice. I told them that if I was only able to depend on the support of the *Anteo* for a single dive then even though they were all set up for Variable Weight I would prefer it to be a No Limits attempt. However I wanted to make a statement: I wanted to be the first to reach the depth of 150 meters. Everyone looked at me baffled: the record was 138 meters, and a 150 meter dive meant adding twelve meters. Even worse, I hadn't done a No Limits dive since 1996, when I had descended to 131 meters, and I hadn't once practiced the opening of the tank to fill the lift bag on the bottom. But I insisted – I knew I could do it.

The Thursday training session was skipped, and on Friday the *Anteo* took advantage of a light break in the storm, returning to the dive site in front of Portofino. The evening of the 22nd of October we were all on board for the first and last training session before the No Limits attempt. Massimo and I had decided on a dive to 130 meters, which is the depth at which I would need to make the last equalisation, with a thirty second pause on the bottom before filling the balloon: left hand on the handle, right hand turns the lever to open the air bottle, then detaches the lift bag, which pulls me upward again like a hot air balloon. This type of training dive meant we could avoid having to send the deepest safety diver to 150 meters, which would entail an extra two hours of decompression time.

Arriving on board the *Anteo* by five o'clock in the afternoon meant that by the time we had finished all the checks, an hour and a half later, it was already dark and I would have to dive

into pitch blackness and return with the lights of the divers' torches. It was my only chance though, so I had to take it. The sun had long since disappeared over the horizon when I took position on my sled and started the dive. I reached the target depth without any difficulty, stopped and equalised as planned, but realised that I was unable to get any air into my left ear. As much as I pushed, the air wouldn't go in. I tried a third time, almost violently and suddenly heard a loud hissing noise in my left ear. I was surprised, as it was the first time that it had ever happened to me. I waited for the predetermined thirty seconds, made the OK sign to my safety divers, then performed the returning

In the days prior to the No Limits record attempt the weather conditions have prevented me from being able to train. Furthermore I have a ruptured eardrum. However I feel like I am still up to the task – I want to dive to 150 meters. On the surface I concentrate, visualise the dive, and pray. I will do the exact same things during all of the descent.

manoeuvre: left hand on the handle, right hand opens the compressed air tank and detaches the lift bag. I came back to the surface, feeling fine, and was met by my safety freedivers. As soon as I was back on board I called Umberto Berrettini, the doctor who had been treating me for several years. I told him about my difficulty equalising at depth and asked him to have a look at my ear. Together with the ship's doctor he took me to the infirmary, where they examined me and told me: "The eardrum itself is a little bit red, but that's only to be expected with all the diving you've been doing…"

They say that no one is a better doctor than yourself. I decided to believe Berrettini, but I still went to bed a little bit worried, with a strange sensation and muffled sounds in my left ear. On Saturday morning the sea was rough again, and the *Anteo* had weighed anchor and returned to port in Genoa: obviously there was nothing to be done that day. The tension built, and with it my anxiety. I decided to make the most of the circumstances, and called Massimo and Doctor Berrettini together. We

went to the hotel pool, where I put my head under the water, equalised my ears, and we all saw bubbles escaping from my left ear. My coach and doctor both went pale. For Berrettini there was no questioning it: my eardrum was ruptured and I should stay completely out of the water. I wouldn't have it though: everything was ready, and the idea of letting it all go and abandoning the attempt at being the first to 150 meters, all for a microscopic hole caused by a stupid mistake, just didn't go down with me. "No Umberto," I said to the doctor, "I can't go home like this. I have to at least try…" In Elba the Pirate had told me about the coral fishermen who dove regularly with ruptured eardrums, keeping one finger in the ear canal. Stathis Haggi didn't even have eardrums, and Mayol described the Polynesian fishermen who practiced 'patia-titia,' spearfishing with balsa goggles and bamboo spears, and who would perforate the eardrums of their children so that they would never have difficulty equalising.

Evidently there were many freedivers who dove with damaged eardrums, and I wanted

The exit from the 150 meter world record dive on the 24th October, 1999. Two of the surface safety divers, Roberto Chiozzotto and Davide Carrera, are approaching to celebrate with me. My safety scuba divers are still under the water: the deepest have another five hours of decompression time ahead of them.

I'm on the bridge of the *Anteo*, surrounded by the journalists and television crews who came for the event. The scale of the organisation is dizzying. Between one interview and another I think back to my beginnings on the island of Elba, where in order to train I had to go to sea in a little rowboat.

to find out what would happen to me. Doctor Berrettini warned me about thermal shock, which can have traumatic effects. We decided on an attempt for the next day, Sunday the 24th. The conditional as always was the weather. Massimo urged me to not think about it, but it was difficult to think about anything else. Every so often I would look out my window to see if I could spot the *Anteo's* lights out at sea, but I couldn't see anything. Finally, by the evening the reassuring shape of the ship materialised offshore from Portofino: the captain had decided to take advantage of the second gap between the storms, and the relative calm that always came with nightfall in order to anchor the boat as well as possible, with the intention of attempting the dive early the next morning.

For me this was an incredibly important dive, but it promised to be one of the most psychologically difficult: I had never attempted a record in this state. I had trained very little in No Limits, I had one ruptured eardrum, and I had no idea what was in store for me beyond 130 meters. However I had nothing to lose: I could count on the *Anteo* and a perfect organisation, and I certainly wouldn't let a tiny hole in an eardrum stop me. Most importantly I thought about all the sacrifices I had made, for so many years, when I was practically a nobody, and I felt that it

was very important for me to reach this goal of 150 meters, 12 meters deeper in a single dive – the most in the history of freediving records. It was a long, interminable night for me. My alarm was set for 5 a.m., and by 5:30 we were at the port. We were using enormous reinforced inflatable dinghies, with powerful outboard motors, but to reach the *Anteo* only a few miles away took us all of an hour, when it would normally take minutes. The port side of the ship was being hit by four meter high waves. Massimo advised me to climb up on to the top deck, concentrate on my breathing and relaxation and think as positively as possible. The team started work on setting the descent line, given to the ship's captain by the judges and notaries who had checked and measured it.

Video cameras are positioned, ready to be activated. At 10 o'clock I am told to come down to the bridge to put on my wetsuit and begin the final phase of preparation before the dive. I can read the concern in the eyes of Massimo and the doctor – they are the only people who know about my perforated eardrum. I can feel that all the men of my team are tense: they know I haven't reached this depth before and that I am untrained in No Limits. The only thing which reassures them is the recent world record in Constant Weight, but 150 meters is almost twice as deep. I was able to relax well up

on the top deck of the *Anteo*: most of the time I spent telling myself that I had nothing to lose and that I only needed to try and do what I could, even if that meant reaching a new limit, and that I must go slowly with the broken eardrum.

Before I enter the water Doctor Berrettini comes close to me and says, "Take care Umberto – don't do anything that might harm you permanently. If you feel pain, stop the sled and come back up." I wink and tell him not to worry. I skip my normal warm-up dive, and instead do a simple four-minute static apnea on the surface before climbing onto the sled. I give the five-minute signal, and Gigi starts calling out the countdown. At zero I give the signal to detach the sled. I am lightly squeezing the brake in order to slow the descent speed slightly. On the way down I lift the edge of my hood a little to allow water into my ear so that I can avoid the thermal shock that was Berrettini was so concerned about. I descend slowly to about 3-4 meters, then tell myself, "OK Umberto, now you're going to have to try this out." I blow tentatively against my blocked nose, and both ears equalise correctly, even if a few bubbles of air leak out from the damaged eardrum. I'm happy. "You have eight litres of air in your lungs," I tell myself, "it's not like you're going to empty them with a trickle of bubbles from your ears." I open the brake and let myself drop towards 150 meters.

It is one of the most beautiful dives of my life. On the bottom the *Anteo's* winged ROV is waiting for me, and Massimo and Alberto wave to me, and watch me a little worried. I give them a nod to say that everything is go-

A group photo with the hard hat divers of the *Anteo*. The Italian navy supplied me and my team with the best conditions to work in maximum safety. I will never forget the professionalism and affection demonstrated by the whole of their team.

150 meters, and I am extremely proud of this – it is an event that will be remembered forever. Depths between 50 and 100 are quickly forgotten, as are those between 100 and 150, but the 'historic' depths will always be remembered, and 150 meters is definitely one of those. It is a milestone on the road into the great abyss, reached on the 24th of October 1999.

We remained on the *Anteo* for several hours while the divers decompressed, some of them for as long as five hours. Some of my deep safety divers have never seen me surface after a record, since they have always been under the water decompressing. I returned to the water to greet and thank all of them, shaking each one tightly by the hand.

The weather conditions continued to be prohibitive to further diving, and there was no chance for the Variable Weight record. In any case I had already decided: before I hung my fins up on a peg on the wall I wanted to complete my set of three world records. There was only one left, Variable Weight, but it would have to wait until 2001, since for 2000 I was committed to the filming of an Imax film, *Ocean Men*, which tells the story of me and Pipin, our records, rivalries and our relationships with the sea. So the final chapter is delayed until 2001.

A tearful moment with my mother, Maria. Her warm embrace and tears accompanied every one of my records, and she wanted to be there for this historic dive also: Maiorca was first to reach 50 meters, Mayol the first to 100 and I, her son, was first to 150.

ing well. I look around me and find myself in front of the *Anteo's* ROV, which flashes its lights in greeting and in blessing. I imagine the face of the technician on board the *Anteo* who is responsible for controlling the ROV (Remote Operated Vehicle): until that moment at this depth he would have only ever seen one of his peers in a rigid diving suit. Now the video cameras were displaying images of a man without any breathing equipment, his body protected only by a simple neoprene wetsuit. I feel like an ambassador for humanity under the sea. I am the first man to cross the barrier of 150 meters on a breath hold.

Maiorca was the first to reach 50 meters, Mayol the first to 100 and I was the first to

Silver bank: the whalesong

After a brief visit home I left again to finally meet a marine animal that I had not yet seen up close: the whale. I chose the area of sea between the Turks and Caicos and Santo Domingo, at the so-called 'Silver Bank.' The name is derived from a Spanish galleon that sank, laden with treasures, into these shallow waters in 1641. Part of the hoard was recovered by a diving treasure hunter in 1996.

This site is the yearly meeting place for *Megaptera novæangliæ* (humpback whales), who migrate every March from Canada to an area of water about the size of the island of Elba. Scattered coral heads come to just under the surface of the water, and amongst these lies the wreck of the *Kinsei Maru*, a Japanese cargo ship, that went aground about twenty five years ago when fleeing from the US Coast Guard, probably with a cargo of contraband that was certainly neither silver, gold or diamonds. Now it has rusted into a red ghost ship that makes a stunning backdrop to the colours and splendour of the reef life. I reached the bank from Puerto Plata (Santo Domingo), about ninety miles away, on a ten meter boat, intending to stay in the area for a week. All around me there was nothing but sea, broken only by the in-

The graceful movement of a *Megaptera novæangliæ* (humpback whale). I was lucky enough to meet great numbers of these in the waters of the Turks and Caicos islands and Santo Domingo, on the so-called 'Silver Bank.'
These 'great-winged' whales migrate every year in March from Canada all the way to the Caribbean.

congruous shape of the enormous Japanese cargo ship, completely covered in rust, and with the stern submerged. Here I could take advantage of my freediving ability: free from the encumbrance of a scuba tank I could penetrate into the ecosystem inside the ship. I was kept company by the unsettling noise of sheets of metal creaking against each other as they opened and closed like curtains at the theatre: I felt like I was in an old horror film. I would often squeeze into narrow openings, letting myself be pulled in by the current and pushed out by a wave.

In the open water I met with the giants of the sea. As the name 'humpback whale' suggests they weren't exactly beautiful, but the gracefulness of their movements is incomparable, as in all cetaceans. I had already been afforded a couple of sporadic encounters, but here the spectacle was unique. Ten thousand humpback whales arrive every year from Canada to court, mate and reproduce, since if their only child were to be born in the arctic sea the fatty layer of its skin wouldn't be sufficient to keep it warm in the freezing water.

Their brawny tails that flatten waves and the plumes of spray created by their exhales give an idea of the power of these animals – even more so their incredible leaps out of the water to seemingly impossible heights. Then there was the amazing display put on by the big males: slicing through the water like battling submarines, they chased each other, shoved each other, surfaced quickly and crowded together around a single female, which was probably giving off signals of being in heat. The first time I entered the water I wasn't completely at ease. It's not that I was scared, but it was the first time I had ever found myself in a similar situation: in the middle of the blue open ocean, so close to these giants, I became aware of my physical insignificance in that environment. I, who am by no means small, felt the breath of a living creature eight times longer than I am and many more times as heavy. It was an incredible sensation that flooded my body and nervous system with adrenalin. I had to be as agile as a dolphin in order to avoid

At the start of the training season, several months before competitions, I don't think about the records or adversaries I have to beat, or the rope I will have to follow, but instead I live in the sea, trying to create in every dive a more vivid and emotive experience than the last. I relax every part of my body, imagine an internal music, and begin to move as elegantly as possible to its rhythm. The freedive becomes like a dance: an expression of my body and emotions.

being swept aside. If I wanted to get close then I had to anticipate the movement of a whale by its trajectory: I would see it heading in a certain direction and move to intercept it with the boat's tender, then jump in the water and wait for the whale to arrive. The most intriguing moment of these encounters was when the enormous white fins materialised from the blue, moving towards me. They are what give the species its Latin name *mega* (large) *ptera* (wings), and can reach a length of up to five meters. Straight away the rest of the animal would emerge from the blue, lumbering towards me, before passing underneath me and continuing on its way. The first sighting sent tingles up my spine, and after a week I'd had numerous encounters. I remember especially the baby whales, who would leave their mother's side to come and look at us curiously. The mothers would turn around to retrieve them and take them away, holding them with their lateral fins as they moved off from the intruders with powerful strokes of their tail flukes.

Once, while I was inside the Japanese wreck, I saw a beautiful scene: a humpback whale was swimming together with four dolphins who were playing by her side. It was a beautiful sight to behold, especially framed as it was: the porthole opening onto the pure blue and immensity of the ocean. I would normally dive in the evenings, when the sun was low on the horizon, and I would use the chain of the *Ocean Explorer* to pull myself down to the bottom. There, at about 10-15 meters I would hold my breath and wait to be pervaded by the whales' song. These calls are a speciality of humpback whales, especially of the males during mating season: the longer they are able to sing the more likely they are of finding a mate. All cetaceans communicate by sound, but humpback whales are famous amongst researchers, who dive with microphones into their watery concert halls to record the sounds and create sonograms. But to swim alongside them and listen with your own ear to their mysterious voices, amplified by the liquid element, makes your hair stand on end.

Ocean Men

The world of freediving was in constant development: it was no longer a 'two horse race' between myself and Pipin, and there were always new names and other strong athletes. New disciplines were being added to the sport also, such as 'static apnea,' a very difficult discipline psychologically, in which the athlete has to stay immobile as long as possible in the water without breathing, and 'dynamic apnea,' where the athlete has to swim as far as possible horizontally in a swimming pool: a discipline that isn't quite as difficult mentally, but which makes up for it physically. 'Free immersion' also began to take off, and in this discipline the freediver can use the descent line to pull themselves down and up, but cannot use fins or any other assistance. However it was in Constant Weight that the biggest changes were happening: the use of monofins had been approved, and after the year 2000 they quickly substituted the traditional 'bi-fins' in most competitions and record attempts. So my last record in the discipline, the 80 meter dive of the 18th October 1999, was the last record using long carbon bi-fins. The introduction of the monofin was an important event, since the record in Constant Weight quickly passed to 85 meters and deeper.

When I returned from the encounters with the whales I started out on another unique experience: Pipin and I had been chosen by the German production company H5B5 to star in an Imax film called *Ocean Men*. The film aimed

to be an Imax version of *Le Grand Bleu (The Big Blue)*, by Luc Besson, which set box office records in world cinema. The new film would tell the parallel stories of Pipin and I, men of the ocean: Pipin discovered the sea before he even learnt to walk (he says that sacrifices were made in his name to Olocun, the supreme god of the seas, in a Santeria ceremony on the beaches of Cuba); I came to the sea by a completely different route, terrorised underneath the shower or in the swimming pools of Busto Arsizio.

They had planned on eighteen months of filming in order to finish the piece. I was called on immediately for the first part of filming in South Andros in the Bahamas. In the heart of the forest that covers the island, which is the biggest in the archipelago of the Bahamas,

there is a chasm full of water, and we were supposed to dive in the middle of it. I was positioned standing on the edge of the hole, ten meters above the body of murky black water, covered with leaves and looking like a little bit like a bog. The hole opens out into a cylindrical shaft 120 meters deep. They call it Stargate, and diving there is no easy matter. In the first 10-12 meters you can't see anything – the water is green, and the rays of light make surreal weaving patterns. However after those first few meters the water becomes like crystal, and rather than swimming it almost feels like you are flying through air. It's a little like science fiction films where a man reaches out his hand and passes through a wall: in this case you open the gate to the stars and enter into complete transparency, dotted with white stalactites and stalagmites that reflect the light of your torch, filling the whole chamber with light. It was one of the most fantastic freedives in my life.

I insisted that the production company come to Sardinia to see Capo Testa, and how I lived and trained: I was proud of my Italian and Mediterranean origins, and I wanted this to be evident in *Ocean Men*. The film crew spent a month there, and were blown away by the beauty of the place. I even succeeded in getting Jacques Mayol to come and visit and have a role in the production: he opens the film, telling the history of freediving. The director Bob Talbot was a very famous photographer, and as we explored Capo Testa he confessed to understand my life choices and my insistence on using that location: he said he had seen very few places which matched its beauty.

I escape to Capo Testa whenever I need to relax and concentrate. For me it is the most beautiful corner of Sardinia, and definitely the most meaningful to me, a place where I have

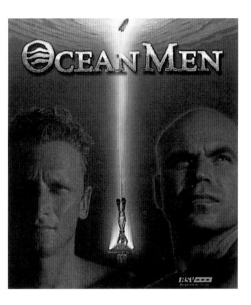

The poster for the Imax film *Ocean Men*, which told the story of Pipin and I: our histories, our different ways of approaching the sea and our rivalry.

I am breathing amongst the magical rocks of Capo Testa.

chosen to spend the most difficult moments of my sporting career. I go there to concentrate, to look at the sea and to talk to it. I get angry with the sea, and on some occasions I may even hate it. But I always return straight away to love the sea, and I realise that I could never live without it. I admire the strength that the ocean displays even when seen from the outside, the waves that change shape in every fraction of a second, and I realise that the sea is communicating with me. However Capo Testa is chiefly the place where I escape to when I want to talk with the departed Tore: from the granite summits I look out to sea towards the Secca del Diavolo, where Tore disappeared in 1997, and I ask him to stay close to me in my dives.

After Capo Testa we transferred the film crew to the island of Roatan, in Honduras, where we spent two incredible weeks and filmed breath-taking scenes in the company of a pair of dolphins. Filming for Imax is very different to using traditional methods: the film stock is seventy millimeters – twice normal size – and this means that the cameras have to be kept in enormous housings, with very limited mobility. After at most a minute and a half of filming they would have to take everything out of the water, dry the housing, open it and replace the reel with a new one. This allowed me to spend a lot of time in the water with the two dolphins, Pablo and Esteban, and to play with them even when we weren't required for the filming.

I always tried to put into practice the advice of Mayol, and to experience new and beautiful sensations in each freedive. I knew of course that I had to train for the Variable Weight record on the horizon, but I didn't want to think about depths and times yet – I was interested only in being as aquatic as possible, being aware of myself in the water and registering new and stronger sensations. I was with the two dolphins for eight to ten hours of the day. They were wild dolphins, but accustomed to the presence of humans, and we were able to build a special bond since I was able to play with them in ways others couldn't. I studied them closely, keeping in mind what Mayol always told me, that when we enter the water we must forget about our human laws and adopt those of the sea, and who better to teach us those

laws than the dolphin, which like us is an air-breathing mammal, but who lives in the sea… This is why I have always watched the behaviour, patterns of movement and the elegance of these small cetaceans. Dolphins have been my greatest teachers under the water, and it was the same in Roatan: I tried to imitate Pablo and Esteban in everything they did underwater. I tried to understand how much I still needed to learn, especially in view of my record attempt programmed for 2001.

In order to film the television version of *Ocean Men* we travelled to China. Jacques Mayol, who was born in Shanghai, had spoken to me also of the Shaolin. They are a community of monks who live in the valley of the Temple of Henan, an area in the heart of China, and crossed by seven hundred kilometers of the Yellow River (*henan* means 'south of the river'). The area is only a hundred and seventy thousand square kilometers, making it one of the smallest provinces of China, but with over ninety million inhabitants it is also one of the most densely populated. From Peking it took us two and a half hours by plane to reach Zheng Zhou, the capital of the province, and from there three hours by road brought the film crew to the Valley of Temples.

After the filming had finally finished I decided to stay alone by myself with these Buddhist monks, who take their name from what is still today the most famous school for the techniques of kung fu – the greatest of the Chinese martial arts. There are in fact as many different schools as there are styles of kung fu, and they are divided into two main groups: those that deal with the most violent combat, such as Shaolin-bai, Hongjia-pai, Zhong-pai, Chuk-kai-quan, and the 'softer' styles such as Taiji-quan and Bagua-pai. Kung fu dates back almost three thousand years, but it wasn't until the second century AD that a famous teacher called Kuo-I created a style called Ch'ang Shou that most consider to be the main predecessor to the Shaolin.

In the Valley of Temples there are a multitude of youths, even four to ten year old children, who live in academies connected to the temples and study kung fu in order to become Shaolin

We can always learn
something from
encounters with
the inhabitants of
the seas. The most
important thing is
to forget about our
human nature and
athletic performance.
We must let ourselves
go and feel the
lightness that water
gives to our bodies.
The true freediver is
the one who doesn't
appear to be using
physical force under
the water. Everything
comes naturally, and
the observer should
think that freediving
is the most simple
activity in the world.

(on the following
pages)
In the waters of
the Caribbean I
enjoy playing with
a sea turtle, a very
docile and easily
approachable animal.

monks, body guards or even actors like Bruce Lee – it's true that they could have even become business managers, given that the temples supplied them with complete physical, mental and spiritual training. The place was rich in history. The first monastery was constructed with the consent of the emperor Xiaowen in the year 495 AD by the Indian monk Batuo, who was responsible for the diffusion of Buddhism in the Chinese Empire. Even so, only thirty two years later, in 527 AD, another Indian monk called Bodhidarma settled in the valley and founded Chinese Buddhism, introducing the idea that the practice of martial arts contributed to the harmonious development of body and spirit. The Shaolin have been able to preserve the essence of their culture down through the centuries, and it's a culture that is deeply rooted in its society, enabling it to pass almost unscathed through the upheaval of the cultural revolution lead by chairman Mao Zedong.

The young would-be monks pass the days at their studies, trying to understand the essence of chi (or qi), the vital energy present in air, in nature, and in great uncontaminated spaces: it is a word that has more than seventeen different meanings. 'Gong' on the other hand can mean 'continuous regular training,' and so *qi gong* would mean 'control of vital energy.' In order to apprehend and utilise the positive effects of *qi* one must first eliminate all physical tension and mental stress as well as learn how to control breathing. So the students must learn the soft and coordinated way of movement manifested in the movement of Tai Chi, the very slow type of gymnastics which is itself a traditional Chinese martial art founded on the duality of *yin* and *yang*, and which applies active relaxation, sequences of coordinated movements and the development of energy.

These disciplines fascinated me, especially the techniques of breath control that the Shaolin use to eliminate negative thoughts and purify their spirit. Jacques Mayol would tell me that breathing is very difficult to teach: from birth we learn to breathe poorly, utilising only the thorax and thus only the upper part of the lungs. To take advantage of our respiratory potential we must bring into play the lower part of the lungs, and learn how to move the diaphragm: upwards in order to completely empty the lungs, and downwards to fill them. Jacques introduced me to techniques of *pranayama*, but now I wanted to see how the Shaolin monks breathed. I was admitted into a group of youngsters being guided by an old master. He looked like he must have been seventy years old, and of the two paths that a monk is required to choose between at the start of their lives – contemplation or combat – my master had chosen the second. He walked lightly, supporting himself with a stick, but when he fought he was transformed: his movements acquired lightning rapidity and the walking stick became a lethal weapon. I spoke at length with him, using an interpreter. He told me that *qi* came from the sun, and needed big open spaces in order to dispense its energy. The monk alluded to the great valleys in which we find ourselves, but I was thinking that the infinitely more vast space of the oceans might allow for an even greater *qi*. The master explained to me that one had to succeed in allowing the *qi* to enter and become part of our bodies, but that this could only come through years and years of unshakeable conviction and intense daily practice of

the techniques of breathing, concentration and relaxation. In the days I spent with the monk he tried to identify any contraction during the phases of my breathing, and he taught me to relax and look always to the sun. He gave me basic breathing exercises that I realised I was unable to perform, and tried to increase my sensitivity to the movement of the diaphragm, and thereby my ability to work with the lower parts of the lungs, which are the most voluminous and important. But the most valuable thing he taught me was that with willpower and the force of the mind we can do things we would have thought impossible. I watched boys break steel bars over their heads without even suffering a scratch, and children seven years old jumping off tables with a double back flip and landing on their heads, only to jump back up as if nothing had happened.

I was able to take away a couple of things that I could apply to my sport. Since then, whenever I get ready to enter the water for a deep freedive I always breath with the diaphragm, I look in the direction of the sun, and I try to taste the flavour of the air that I am sucking inside of me – the vital energy which invigorates and prepares me for the challenge with the abyss and with myself.

The Shaolin are Buddhist monks, and take their name from what is still today the principal school for the teaching of kung fu, the prominent of the Chinese martial arts. They live in the Valley of Temples in Henan, a province in the centre of China, crossed by seven hundred kilometers of the Yellow River. The Shaolin took me in as if I was one of their own. As a beginner they taught me that in order to make improvements physically and spiritually I would have to live in close contact with nature. The open air, wide spaces and the sun contain the vital energy which would allow me to become an even greater freediver. With a certain type of breathing I would be able to reduce mental stress, and smooth and controlled movements of the whole body would allow me to eliminate muscular tension.

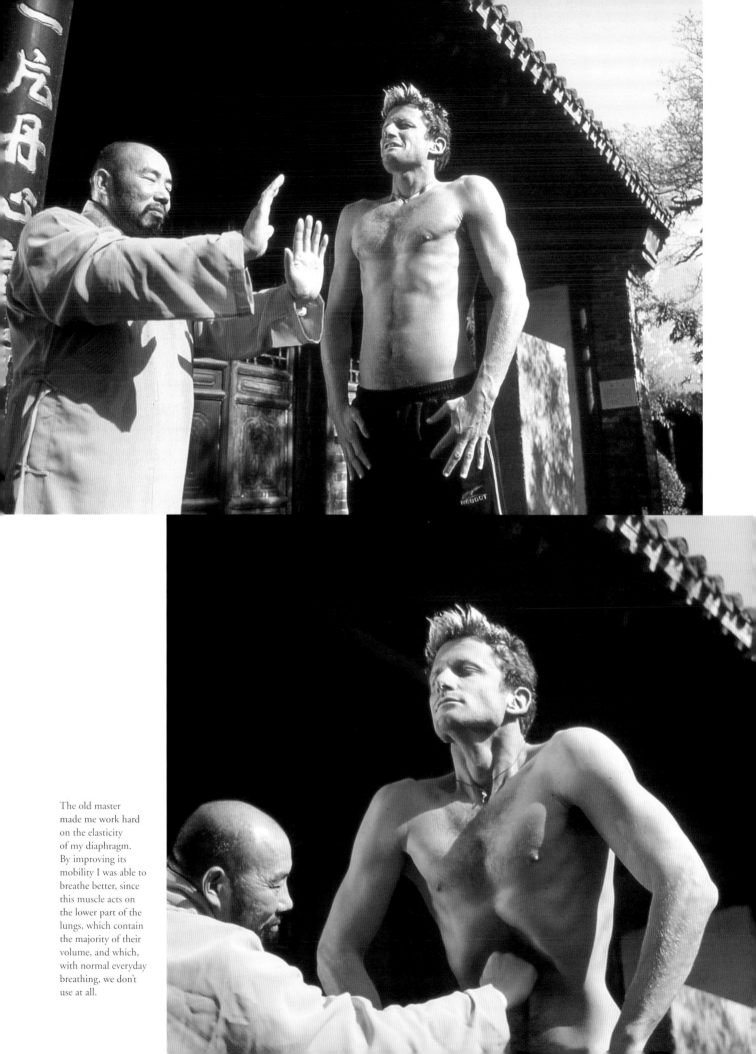

The old master
made me work hard
on the elasticity
of my diaphragm.
By improving its
mobility I was able to
breathe better, since
this muscle acts on
the lower part of the
lungs, which contain
the majority of their
volume, and which,
with normal everyday
breathing, we don't
use at all.

By then it is certain: 2001 would be the last year of my sporting career, and I wanted to prepare for my final event in the best possible way. Sardinia would allow me to regain the concentration necessary – whenever I was feeling stressed I could take refuge amongst the rocks of Capo Testa, and there I would rejuvenate. What's more, with my friend Tommasino I had opened a diving centre, and my freediving school, the Apnea Academy, was creating more instructors and propagating its teaching methods. I stayed in Sardinia until the end of August, then I left to participate in the world premiere of *Ocean Men* in Monaco di Baviera. I saw Mayol there, and he was acting strangely, as if he had aged psychologically. He alternated between moments of great lucidity and enthusiasm and moments of sullen resignation. "You know," he said to me, "It would be nice if you and I could open a school together, maybe in Elba or in the Bahamas…" Then half an hour later: "Do you see how old and lonely I am? I don't know why God puts us on the planet only to leave us like this." Jacques was always full of enthusiasm and a desire to act and affirm himself, but now he came across as passive and resigned. I sensed that there was something amiss.

Ocean Men enjoyed a great success in the Imax theatres. I came straight back to Elba, where we were due to start training for the third edition of the Freediving Teams World Championships, to be held at the start of October in Ibiza. More than forty countries had entered, and for the first time the teams would be composed of three rather than five athletes, each competing in Constant Weight and static apnea. With me in the team were Gaspare Battaglia and Davide Carrera, who was getting progressively stronger as a freediver. At the start the tension got to us a little, especially in static apnea. We began with the Constant Weight attempts, matching the depths that we had declared in the announcements. They would never be extremely trialling depths – we only ever announced 'safe' depths that we could reach easily, since in a teams competition it would be foolish to attempt records and put the whole team's

During the inhale (above) the diaphragm lowers and air fills first the abdominal zone, then the thoracic zone, and finally the upper zone around the clavicle.
The exhale (below) has the reverse sequence. It starts from the top, working its way to the bottom of the lungs. At the end the diaphragm is raised upwards into the base of the lungs in order to push out residual air.

The Italian men's and women's teams who took part in the Freediving Teams World Championships in Ibiza in October 2001. This event was very important for the development of freediving. It confirmed the tradition and strength of the Italian schools, with gold medals for the men and bronze for the women.

ranking at risk from a blackout and subsequent elimination. In fact the disqualification of just one freediver due to blackout could mean the loss of up to ten positions in the final ranking. In static apnea we knew the French were stronger than us, and our captain, Roberto Chiozzoto told us: "We're going to announce very low times so that we perform first, do our best, and then see what the French are capable of." It would be at the same time an advantage and disadvantage, since if an athlete gets in the water knowing the performance of his rival then on the one hand he knows what time he has to surpass in order to win, but on the other hand it can be psychologically very tough if you know you have to hold your breath for a predetermined amount of time. In our case Roberto's strategy proved to be the winning tactic, since the French, who were normally capable of

over seven minutes, couldn't pull off more than six minutes in the competition. For the third straight occasion we beat the French, with only two points difference between the teams, equal to 10 seconds in static apnea or two meters in Constant Weight. The points system is devised by a conversion between meters and seconds, whereby a meter depth and five seconds in static are both equal to one point, and the team with the highest points aggregate wins.

In Ibiza for the first time the women participated as well, with more than twenty teams. Italy, captained by Andrea Badiello, finished in third place. The victory of the men, and the excellent placing of the women, confirmed once again the value of the Italian schools and teaching methods of the Apnea Academy, which had trained most of the competing athletes.

Davide Carrera and I prepare for the mentally toughest discipline: static apnea. We are very tense, and perform well below our personal bests. Perhaps we are already thinking about the depth records we will be attempting in November in Capri.

Celebration in the pool after the static apnea performances which gave our team victory.

The grand finale

There wasn't even time to celebrate the victory of the Italian team. I had to concentrate immediately on the last event of my sporting career: an attempt at the Variable Weight world record that I'd had to renounce two years earlier in Portofino.

The hosting of the event went to Capri, off the coast of Naples. I would attempt the record on the 3rd of November, when the weather was at its most volatile, with frequent storms, so it was wise to use an island for shelter: if the sea was too rough on one side then we could head to the other side to find calmer seas. Capri is an island of sheer cliffs which continue vertically down below the surface, and so the necessary 150 meters could be found quite close to the coast: a good guarantee for protection from the fickle weather.

There were many other reasons for choosing Capri: one of the most important of them was the fact that the first world record in the history of freediving was set right there in the gulf of Naples, by Raimondo Bucher in 1949, when he dove to 30 meters and took from the

(right)
Even in the donning of my wetsuit I follow a precise ritual, maintaining maximum concentration.

(below)
A photo with Davide Carrera in front of the incredible coastline of Capri. This event would signal the passing of the banner: for me it would be the last record, for Davide it would be his debut in freediving, with the discipline of Free Immersion.

hand of a hard hat diver a parchment held inside a watertight metal cylinder – a gesture that was intended to symbolise the passing of the baton from the old 'copper-head' to the new explorer of the abyss, the freediver.

For me the record would be the conclusion of my competitive career, and would be a little like closing the circle. There was also the insistence of Enrico Lupo, one of my many good friends from the first Apnea Academy course in 1996, who had been trying for years to get me to do something in Naples. Now that he had finally convinced me he got to work making sure everything was organised, with logistical and technical arrangements, contacts to the relevant institutions and press releases. For my last record attempt I wanted to take a step back in time and use the protection of the island instead of huge sophisticated ships like *Anfitrite* and *Anteo*. The marine organisation was entrusted to Capo Gianni and Capo Brunello, tuna fishermen from San Marco di Castellabate. Enrico had often talked to me about them, saying that they were genuine 'sea-wolfs,' men who practically lived on the sea for ten months of the year, and had warm mariner's hearts. He had met them in unusual circumstances, when a storm had torn his little sailboat from its mooring and the fishermen had rescued it moments before it would have been smashed to pieces against the rocks. They spent several days stopping leaks in the hull, and mending as best they could the damage caused by the storm. For all that help they refused to accept any payment, but they did talk him into making a promise to introduce them to Umberto Pelizzari and to have me on board of their fishing vessel. Although they worked extremely hard they were aficionados of the sea and underwater sports, and while chatting with Enrico they had found out about our friendship. "If you introduce us to Umberto that would be sufficient repayment for everything," they had told him. So it was that En-

(above)
On board the Santa Maria everything proceeds as it should. Massimo and the team are working on the equipment to prevent any kind of malfunction.

(left)
Davide applies the contact lenses to my eyes before the dive.

rico took me on board to discuss how we could transform the *Santa Maria*, which until now had been a tuna fishing boat, into a logistic base for a freediving world record attempt, and we became immediate friends. I was blown away by their spontaneity and generosity. In Capri I had a room in the luxury hotel 'Giulio Cesare' at Anacapri, but I preferred to spend the evenings with Gianni and Brunello, eating in the galley of the fishing boat and sleeping in a cabin that was less comfortable but full of the smell of salt and the sea.

Everything went like clockwork. To the team we added Mike Maric, another strong freediver who substituted Roberto Chiozzotto (who couldn't be present for that occasion) alongside Davide Carrera on the surface.

It was my last record attempt, and I was using a new silver sled, streamlined to cut through the water like a knife. I wanted each one of my friends to write a message and sign their names on the metal surface: that way they could keep me company during the long voyage towards the bottom of the sea. For this reason I left the sled on the deck where everyone had access to it, and little by little it gradually filled up with notes and signatures. Afterwards I kept that sled for myself. My sister had written: "Neptune thanks you and says farewell. He will miss you!" and Jorge Rodas: "Don't worry, nobody's going to break the record you have in good spirit…" and another: "Go Umberto! You're one of a kind!" and many many more affectionate messages.

The big day drew near, and as if on cue (as always) the wind picked up on the 2nd of November. On the 3rd the sea was still very choppy, and the boats had to delay going out. We had arranged live coverage with the main Italian television station between 1:30 and 2pm, but every operation involving the anchorage and the connection of electric cables to the video cameras brought new delays. We had to abandon the idea of the live feed and shift everything back by half an hour. Despite the bad weather a horde of spectators had turned out to watch: everyone knew that it was to be my last record, and even if few of them believed it they still wanted to come and see me off.

At 2:27 in the afternoon Gigi detached my sled for the last time. It was a perfect descent to 131 meters. I set off from the bottom with long

(on the previous page)
A training dive with my safety team offshore from Capri. In this kind of situation it's easy to find the right concentration, but everything changes on the day of a record attempt.

(right)
A photo taken moments before my departure towards 131 meters. Thousands of friends, hundreds of boats, judges, photographers, television crews, the pressure of officialness, and the knowledge that there will be no second chance… everything has to go perfectly, right now.

(below)
Here I am with my sister Stefania, who has always been close to me in the moments of greatest tension.

A photo taken during the descent towards 131 meters.

(on the next page)
I have just started the ascent towards the surface, after leaving the sled on the bottom. All my friends and the people who came to Capri to be close to me had written a message for me on the sled. It's almost as if they were all with me during my descent to the bottom of the sea.

pulls on the descent line, each stroke taking me several meters closer to the surface. My eyes were shut but I knew that every time I closed my hand it would be around the rope.

Finally, after two minutes fifty seven seconds I returned to breathe in the wind, holding in my fist the tag that proved my descent to a depth of 131 meters. I had surpassed Gianluca Genoni by five meters, but more importantly I had reached in Variable Weight, with a limited ballast weight and returning to the surface under my own force, the same depth that I had reached in No Limits five years earlier in 1996. The last record was particularly poignant for the men of my team. When, for the last time, I dove down to greet my decompressing safety divers, Massimo came towards me and I saw that his eyes were glistening. I am sure that in that moment he was reliving all the adventures of the last twelve years and the sixteen world records we had set together: he would have many long hours of decompression to remember them all. And when I turned to thank him he embraced me tightly – we knew it would be the last time we met each other in those circumstances. The whole team was sad because our adventures together were coming to an end. We are all still friends and we continue to see each other regularly, but that final attempt was the last time we would share the same emotions that only a new world record can bring. The team, which had grown over the years with the addition of new members, was a model of trust and efficiency in an easy-going climate. Each diver had a nickname: Ivan was the 'Professor;' Samuel was 'Trashman' because of his job as a street cleaner on Elba; Stefano Furgani, the policeman, was of course called 'Inspector;' Corrado, a muscly fire-fighter, was christened 'Popeye;' Daniele was named 'Oxford' due to his posh accent; Luca Bortolus was the 'Philosopher;' Alberto Gnuva was the 'Citizen,' and Gigi was the 'Florentine.'

All good stories have one beginning and one ending… To finish with a world record was the most elegant way I could hope for, and it allowed me to leave an indelible and positive image in the annals of the sport. However that doesn't make it any easier a decision to take, especially since though I finished with a world record I knew that 131 meters was not my limit – that I would have been able to go deeper in

all the disciplines. But then I realised that after sixteen world records my sporting image would have nothing left to gain by a few more similar achievements. I had proved everything I wanted to prove to myself and to my friends. Of course I miss the competitions and record attempts. When you compete at a professional level you become accustomed to living every day with a certain level of stress, and when this sporting stress is taken away it almost seems like you lose a reason for living, a reason for waking up in the morning. This happened to me as well, and the people who were closest to me were aware of it. In this delicate period my sister recognized my disorientation. In the final years she had been the organiser and soul of all my record attempts, and she wrote me a sweet and reassuring letter: "Dear Umby, if for one person the end of a sporting career represents the finish line, for you it is only the beginning! That's right, after years of toil and sacrifice, training and tension, now you can finally allow yourself some well-earned rest. I'm sure that you're only at the beginning of a new and brilliant career that will bring you further successes in different areas, and that will allow you to continue to live with your principal passion – the sea… And in all this I will continue to stay close to you, and to support you unconditionally and without reserve." So I concentrated on other professional projects, such as promoting my school, the Apnea Academy, and this alternative allowed me to continue doing what I loved: living with the sea, in the sea and for the sea.

There's nothing more beautiful for a human being than to succeed in combining your job with your most authentic calling in life, to earn your bread by working passionately with your own passion. For me this is sliding underwater in silence, letting my body be caressed by the sea's blue fingers, and the fact that this is also my occupation makes me fulfilled and happy. I hope that what I do leaves just as lasting an impression in humanity.

My last exit and my last record.
I wanted to savour it for as long as possible. I hugged all my safety divers, showed them the tag, and thanked everyone.
Then for a moment I closed my eyes and though about all my adventures, all my victories, and my journeys and dives in all the seas of the world.

(above)
Here I am with Jorge, Mike and Enrico, trusted
safety freedivers.

(right)
I dive back down to thank my safety divers.
I know that this will be the last time that I
descend to shake their hands, and while I was
down there I could see tears welling inside their
masks. We shared many beautiful and intense
moments, and we will surely never forget them.

Jacques and I in a light-hearted moment.

Mayol takes his leave

Since ending my competitive career I'm now busy with other important projects: filming underwater videos and documentaries, and hosting television programs, which allow me – in the same way they did for Jacques Mayol – to transmit my experience and passion to the next generation, and perhaps to incite a degree of nostalgia in the older folk. Most importantly I want to push forward the Apnea Academy, which is showing great potential.

I am aware of the fact that I am very privileged, since the secrets of deep freediving were revealed to me by none other than Jacques Mayol. Now I have one objective: to transmit all my learning through teaching and practical guidance to whoever wants to practice freediving in a certain way, in order to go underwater with greater ease, pleasure and safety.

After the record in Capri I spent several days at home with my parents in Busto Arsizio. Only a fortnight had passed when I already felt a strong need to return to the sea. In December the Pirate called me on the phone, saying "Umberto, if you can, come to Elba for a while – Mayol isn't doing so well. I think it might help him a bit if you spent some time here." Of course I left straight away. I met with Jacques, and found myself in the presence of an almost empty man, without any kind of stimulus. Even the previous August, at Monaco di Baviera when we had screened the premier of *Ocean Men,* he seemed different to the Mayol I knew: apathetic, unsatisfied and uncertain. Nevertheless every so often he had proposed that we do something together, such as a freediving school, even if he soon fell back to depression afterwards. Now these flashes of interest, these simulacrum of enthusiasm had completely disappeared. In front of me was a disheartened man, tired of living, and probably scared by the idea of aging, who had realised that those people who he had thought of as his friends had behaved that way only out of opportunism. Jacques had lived the last twenty years of his life as a full celebrity: in France he was an idol, and his fame had been fed by the huge success of *The Big Blue*. It was clear that he found it difficult to consider any kind of decline from this. In the three days that we spent together I tried to get him talking and to convince him that he didn't have any problems, and was doing fine. One day, while we were chatting he looked me straight in the eyes and said, "You know, I've had incredible experiences with my records and my life in the sea… but I think my most intense and important experience still awaits me." I never imagined what he was alluding to, but I deciphered that message a week later. I had to leave after only three days in Elba, because I was due to set off again for Brazil, where I would be filming a documentary on the Amazon river. As soon as I arrived in Rio on the 23rd of December 2001 I called home and my sister gave me the news: "Mayol committed suicide."

The Pirate had found him that same day in his house in Capoliveri. He had hung himself, leaving a message of farewell and apology to all his friends. According to Alfredo, the knot on the noose had been tied like a work of art, so he was definitely lucid when he killed himself.

It was a difficult action to explain, especially for a person such as Jacques, who in order to earn a living had been a woodsman, pianist, interpreter, actor, journalist, and in the last twenty years he had 'suppressed the primary instinct' to breathe, diving into the abyss. Jacques Mayol, born a Frenchman in Shanghai on the 1st of April 1927, had spent long periods meditating with the Shaolin, and he had mastered disciplines of yoga and self-control as well as techniques of breathing.

When I first heard the news of the tragedy my first reaction was anger: "What were you thinking, Jacques? You gave me all the treasures of your knowledge but you weren't able to use that same powerful mental arsenal to defend yourself from the desire to destroy yourself!"

And then what a way to take your own life! The idea of seeing him hanging from the ceiling of his house was the worst ending I could imagine. I would have understood more if he had dived to the bottom of the sea, clinging to a heavy stone, as if the ocean, that had given him so much, had now decided to take him back for itself…

Then the pity started to move in me, and my mind overflowed with memories of Mayol's beautiful stories of the Philippine fishermen and the inhabitants of the Turks and Caicos. Everything he had told me, the secrets he had revealed, his advice, and his being a wise master who gradually bequeathed his wisdom into the open minds of his young disciples – it all came back to me. I recalled what he told me the first time we met: "If you want to dive with me, let go of everything that belongs to your human identity, and take off your dive watch. You mustn't have any objective but this one: every time you dive, every time you reach the bottom of the sea, you must savour sensations that are a little stronger and a little more beautiful than the previous time. You must get right to the bottom of these sensations, and to do so you have to stop caring about the number of meters or seconds."

Mayol in Santa Teresa di Gallura, a year before his death, photographed in a moment that seems to foreshadow solitude and melancholy. Mayol was a life teacher for me, as well as a coach, friend and role model. He forged me as a freediver, and made me understand the real philosophy of freediving. Now I like to imagine him swimming freely in his own sea.

I was often unable to interpret his suggestions, and then I would realise that what seemed at first glance to be something straightforward and almost stupid did in fact have a precise meaning, closely tied to the sensations. To convince me of the importance of breathing and relaxation during preparation for a deep dive, Jacques continued to tell me that a performance didn't start with the duck dive at the beginning of the dive, but long before, even prior to getting in the water. This sort of advice annoyed me at first, but I soon realised that it was all true. Mayol never gave me technical advice, for example on how to swim correctly or equalise, or the right position during a descent – he always talked with me about the psychological component of freediving rather than the physical aspect of performance. I always enjoyed his theatrical character, like a prophet who didn't dispense his knowledge through direct affirmations but rather through messages that had to be interpreted individually. And the nights I spent listening to his stories, the evenings when we would experiment with breathing techniques while watching the sun go down behind Montecristo… the jabs he would give me when I tried to contract my diaphragm and he told me I was too tense – I had to let go more… his attempts to get me to relax my neck and shoulders, which according to him were too rigid: all things which helped me and which turned me into a unique freediver. Because he himself, Jacques Mayol, was unique…

"Believe in the power of your dreams and they'll become reality," he told me. He often spoke about dreams, and in his stories dreams came up often.

Once, when we were together in Monaco, I had said to him jokingly, "You know Jacques, the next record will be my last. I'm giving it up. I'm starting to get old," he had looked at me and replied, "A man becomes old when his memories begin to outnumber his dreams." This had lead me to believe that he was still with us, that he still had a will to live, until out of the blue came the news of his suicide.

In the months that followed my retirement from competitions I dedicated myself to several business projects. The most important of these was the Apnea Academy – a school which would allow me to continue doing what I loved most, living from the sea, in the sea and for the sea. There is nothing more beautiful for a man than to be able to combine his career with his greatest passion, earning his daily bread while working doing what he loves.

To be able to slide silently underwater, letting my body be caressed by the sea's blue fingers, is a payment in happiness for me. I hope that what I am now doing will leave a memory that is just as enduring to humanity as the story of my records.

Beyond Apnea Academy, I have many other ideas and dreams that I am working to forge into realities, such as producing video documentaries on the world's most beautiful diving locations, and hosting television programs, which allow me to transfer my experience and passion to the younger generation while perhaps inducing a little nostalgia in the older folk, in the same way that Jacques did before me.

I am conscious of the fact that I was privileged by the secrets revealed to me by none other than Jacques Mayol. Now I have a single aim: to transfer all my understanding, practical experience and knowledge to whomsoever desires to freedive in a safer, more fun and more pleasurable way.

And so began my time of adventure-travel, with training mixed in. I was diving in the Amazon river to document some very special encounters. I learnt that piranhas, those fish from horror movies, were dangerous only in certain situations: when the river was swollen from rain and escapes from its banks to fill every available hole, turning them into small ponds. After, when the river returns to its normal dimensions, the piranhas remain trapped, without anything left to prey on, and become aggressive to any living thing. In the Amazon river I was able to dive with the pink dolphins called 'inia.' They have very primitive eyes, since sight is more or less worthless in those muddy rivers, and their skin is coloured a delicate pastel rose that shines out in the greenish water. The colour is due to a very shallow blood circulation – at these latitudes cetaceans have to stay cool rather than stay warm like their cousins in the oceans, so they had dis-

The monofin has allowed the freediver to move in a style more similar to that of the dolphin. It is a very difficult piece of equipment to use, but at the same time it is very powerful. After my 80 meter world record in Constant Weight with two fins, all the strongest freedivers in the world started to use monofins. The wall of 100 meters, which was completely inconceivable with traditional 'bi-fins', has been greatly surpassed.

Here I am with Marco Circosta, after a spearfishing trip together. Spearfishing is a noble art. Difficult and demanding, it requires patience and sacrifice: you can spend entire days without catching a single fish. Spearfishing has been a fundamental part of my freedive training.

pensed with any subcutaneous fat stores in order that their blood might flow as close as possible to the water. The first one I met I dedicated to Mayol. "Observe the dolphins as much as you can," he had often told me, "Follow them, listen to them and imitate them. Let them teach you how to live in the water."

I had no more competitive appointments on the horizon, but I couldn't wait to return to Sardinia to spearfish and train. When I finally reached my 'retirement house' in Santa Teresa di Gallura I started practicing with a monofin and feeling my way into the technique. The new device was very appealing to me. When I had attempted records in Constant Weight the French had recommended it to me, but I was too accustomed to the traditional bi-fins… and then of course I would have never taken advice to do with freediving from one of the rival French! Now however I realised that the monofin had incredible potential: it was diffi-

cult to use but allowed for much greater performances, with an elegance of movement and unique aquaticity. Most of all it made it easier to imitate the movement of a dolphin. Mono-fins had been used in finswimming since the beginning of the fifties, when the Hungarian butterfly swimmer Tumpek had substituted the traditional breaststroke kick with an undulation of the legs (the dolphin kick) that was more exhausting, but also a lot faster.

I learnt how to use the monofin for a laugh, enjoying changing between all the positions, such as swimming on my back and brushing the surface of the water, or swimming just beneath the surface without ever coming out of the water, just like a dolphin. I worked hard, and enthusiastically with the new piece of equipment, and was able to reach depths that I had never been to in the official Constant Weight records: recently, without any special training or the scheduled tables that I used for record attempts, I calmly reached the depth of 100 meters! I trained mostly with Marco Circosta, a man I had met during one of my courses in France and had become good friends with. In a way he had taken the place of Francesco Boni and Salvatore, although their memories were indelible. Marco was a great freediver and spearfisher, and we shared many great experiences hunting and freediving. He still has to mature, especially psychologically, but he has the performance to make a name for himself in competitions and depth records.

On the 12th of October 2002 I received another tragic piece of news – the death of Pipin's wife, Audrey Mestre, a twenty eight year old French girl. Audrey had met Francisco in Mexico, during one of his record attempts. She had followed him in both life and sport, becoming herself an exceptional freediver. On that day, the same day of the year that America had been discovered, she was the one who was involved in an attempt to dive to 170 meters, in the waters off the coast of the beach 'La Romana' in the Dominican Republic.

Pipin and I hadn't talked to each other for a long time, and our relationship was far from idyllic. But this new disaster, after the tragedies of Francesco, Tore and Jacques, hit me hard. I decided to write a letter to Pipin, not for mere formality, but to express my sincere sorrow. He and I both knew that all freedivers are part of a big family, and when one is lost everyone is hurt equally. Pipin received my e-mail, was moved by it, and called my sister to ask for my telephone number. He called me the same evening that I was in Liguria with the whole team to safety for Davide Carrera, who was about to attempt a new record.

We were at dinner when the phone rang, and I heard Pipin's voice on the other end. We started to speak, and I told him how sorry I was for the accident that had cost the life of his Audrey. He was choking desperately as he said, "Audrey's dream was that you and I might go diving together like we once did. It's something that I must do for her," he concluded. "I agree," I replied, and I promised him that as soon as we had the opportunity I would do everything possible to meet with him and discuss an event that would be worthy of the memory of Audrey.

Pipin together with his wife Audrey Mestre. In the first interview that Pipin gave after the tragic loss of his wife on the 12th of October 2002 he said, "I lived for two reasons, Audrey and the sea. Now that she is gone, all I have left is the sea, and it will be the sea that brings me back to her."

In 2003 Marco and I travelled together to Martinique for a series of deep dives with the monofin. We reached extraordinary depths, significant improvements in Constant Weight. The barrier of 100 meters didn't seem too distant any more. It wasn't just in Constant Weight that we were surprising ourselves. I was able to reach impressive times in static apnea as well, probably because I no longer had the stress of record attempts and competitions. There in Martinique, while training with Marco, I managed to hold my breath for almost eight minutes – 7'58" to be exact. When I lifted my head out of the water I expected to receive compliments from Marco, but instead he scolded me, saying, "Couldn't you stay just another couple of seconds?! That way you could have done eight minutes clean, and you wouldn't have to think about it again…"

When I returned from Martinique the producers from the Mediaset TV company contacted me, proposing that I host a primetime program called *Sai perché ('Do you know why?')*, a kind of scientific documentary series. I would co-host the program with a girl called Barbara Gubellini, and I would be covering the marine topics while she would deal with those on land. The idea appealed to me, as I wouldn't have to be closed inside a studio, but instead I could be working outdoors and underwater. I also believed that this new activity would give me the possibility to communicate my great passion to others, and introduce them to the incredible sensations that freediving transmits. After a few months I was also given a slot in the program *Pianeta Mare (Sea Planet)*, which afforded me a great satisfaction: to put spearfishing on television, and finally after so many years to bring this sport to fruition and into the public eye.

For me all of this meant travelling around the world and living incredible experiences: from encounters with sharks in the Red Sea to the great white sharks in the big bays of Cape Town, in South Africa. This beautiful but terrifying sea monster is a genuine war machine. It has incredibly developed senses, in particular its sense of smell. It can smell out a single drop of blood dis-

I have finished my sporting career, but the sea continues to be my life. I host television programs that deal with the sea, and film documentaries, as well as develop my school, the Apnea Academy, and I continue to freedive, both for training and for pleasure, in seas all over the world.

solved in five hundred million drops of water. Its teeth, which grow continuously for all of its life, are edged like razors, and arranged into multiple parallel rows, that splay outwards and allow for the immediate substitution of a damaged tooth. The most memorable dive with these complex and fascinating creatures was in South Africa, at Cape Point. There the fishermen of the village Klein Baai have gone into business taking divers out to see the great white sharks, *Charcharodon carcharias*. They call them 'white pointers,' or sometimes even 'white death.' The fishermen tow out a shark resistant cage behind their boats, anchoring next to an island, where long vine-like tendrils of seaweed waved in the current like a thick head of green hair. Many of these marine vines grew all the way to the surface from a depth of twenty meters, their foliage protruding from the water – the tops of trees that are as flexible as grass.

The fishermen started to chum the waters, throwing sardine heads and the bloody scraps from bigger fish into the water. Soon the great white sharks started to arrive and circle round the boat. Now was the time to get in the water (inside the cage of course) and witness the incredible spectacle of these powerful animals as they rubbed themselves against that fragile-looking shelter and crashed their mouths into its metal bars. The cage was a parallelepiped a meter and a half square by three meters high, made from thick iron bars that were set slightly more apart at the center of each face so that photographers wouldn't be obstructed. The largest of the sharks were five and a half meters long – the largest great white shark ever caught was an eight meter female, taken in Malta just after she had given birth. To provoke the predators the fishermen threw tuna and sardine heads into the water, tied to the end of a rope. When a shark neared the bait the fishermen would pull the line in quickly, and the beast would become frustrated and more aggressive. Furthermore we were in an area where the water was very cloudy: visibility was a maximum of two or three meters, and we couldn't see the sharks until they appeared sud-

My new occupation allows me to travel all over the world and experience incredible encounters: orcas in Norway, white sharks in South Africa, the crocodiles of Florida, the whales of Hawaii and whale sharks in Madagascar… I am a very lucky man!

Jacques Mayol always
dreamt about the
romantic ideal of
Homo delphinus, a
human being capable
of moving in the
water like a dolphin
and descending
into the abyss with
the same ease and
elegance.

(on the next page)
I watch the sea
and breathe, seated
on a rock at Capo
Testa. From here I
can see the Secche
del Diavolo, where
Tore and I often
spearfished together.

A great white
shark on the hunt.
This animal is also
sometimes called
'white death.'

denly out of the gloom, almost upon us already. Only two or three divers would venture outside the cages, and they did so only when the visibility was very good – at least twenty meters. Otherwise the shark would appear too quickly and the men wouldn't be able to react with the necessary calm. It is a unique piece of coastline: situated on the extreme southern point of the African continent. The sea is affected by several currents, and the temperature of the water can change rapidly. Diving in an environment so inhospitable due to the seaweed, low visibility and cold made an encounter with such a formidable predator all the more disquieting.

When you see the shark arrive, with movements of incomparable elegance, it is difficult even to perceive that its tail is moving at all. On that day it approached and looked inside my cage, then threw itself against the bars, before returning to the bait, jumping out of the water in its attempt to grab it. Sometimes the

fishermen would wait for the shark to bite a piece of fish before they pulled in the rope attached to it. Here the shark would jump almost completely out of the water in its attempt to retrieve the bait, since it had tasted the fish and didn't want to lose it. It was a spectacle even for the people watching from the boat, who could see right down inside the shark's white throat, as well as all of its three hundred bristling razor-sharp teeth, and, most fascinating of all, the thick white membrane that covers over its eyes to protect them each time it took a bite. Like the point of its nose, the shark's eyes are particularly delicate, and this nictitating membrane prevents them from being wounded by any convulsive movements of its prey.

There were certain sharks that gave an impression of astounding power. We felt small and defenceless inside our cage, and hoped that the animals swimming around us didn't get too animated, as it wouldn't take them much to take it to

pieces. One day a huge great white shark had become infuriated and hurled itself against the bars, where it was caught in the window for photography and filming. It's head had penetrated into this constriction, and become stuck, and the more the animal tried to get away the more of its head was pushed into the cage. Inside the cage were two terrified men, who were staring at the jaws of the shark, just twenty centimeters away from their faces… Luckily they were able to escape from that death trap, and the shark was disentangled also.

At the other end of the world, in Norway, I was able to admire even more powerful predators, no less than hot-blooded mammals. My encounter with the orcas in those freezing seas was even more close and adrenaline-filled than with the great whites. *Orcinus orca*, or 'Killer whales,' as they are commonly known, is in fact the largest member of the dolphin family, growing to over nine meters. It's chilling name is given from the fact that it doesn't just prey on fish, like its smaller cousins, but rather on other sea-mammals, like seals, sea leopards and penguins, depending on whether it is in northern, equatorial or southern waters. It knows how to overturn huge slabs of ice so that its prey slides into the water where it can devour it (in Greenland they documented the extermination of an entire pack of sled dogs in this way), and it doesn't hesitate to swim right up onto a beach in order to seize young sea lions in its jaws. Despite all this there has never been a recorded attack by an orca on a human being. It's a sad fact that all over the world orcas are kept in huge dolphinariums, forced into circus displays for other's enjoyment (something that is of course impossible with sharks).

To enter the open water with wild orcas while they attack an immense school of herrings is an incredible experience. The orcas work as a team: those on the surface stun the fish with powerful slaps of their tails while those underneath feed, then they swap roles and continue… It was an incredible and exhilarating display, but I had to take care to not find myself in the ball of herrings when the orcas brought down their huge tails… I remember that amongst all that confusion I noticed the males had their long dorsal fin completely erect – not like the orcas I had seen in captivity, and not like Stefania when we first saw her…

I met and documented many other intimate encounters with the creatures of the ocean, amongst which the seals of Ireland and the sea lions of the Galapagos – even these pinnipeds are physiologically very similar to humans, and perhaps I could learn secrets from them as well as from the dolphins. Wherever possible, I would try to describe the spirit of Jacques Mayol and his *Homo delphinus*.

In the meantime the Apnea Academy had grown to become the world standard in freediv-

Often during the years in which I attempted world records, when I found myself in difficulty I would ask myself if I shouldn't just give it all up. From within I always heard the answer: "Keep going, it's not yet time to stop." It's the same voice which one day told me: "That's enough Umberto!" I listened to it then as well. It was difficult to retire after having just set a world record, however it was also the most elegant way of doing it. Every beautiful story has one beginning and one ending. It was right to finish it in that way.

ing instruction. There are now several hundred instructors in Italy alone, and another hundred throughout the world, across all the continents. All of them are drawing thousands of people to the fantastic world of freediving, and this is a great satisfaction for me.

I have also written several textbooks: the general Manual of Freediving, a beginner's guide, a manual on breathing techniques and another on freediving training. I currently train instructors and hold freediving courses all over the world so that in every part of it there will be men and women who can act as guides to the underwater world.

I conducted studies to refine the technique of movement with the monofin. I believe that the strongest freediver isn't just the one who goes the deepest, but rather he or she who is able to express the greatest elegance, aquaticity, and imitation of the dolphin. I believe that when we go underwater we should be accompanied by an imaginary music, and we should fly, dance and glide to its rhythm. Anyone watching this ideal freediver shouldn't notice any intensity of movement in the finstroke, but rather the naturalness and fluidity of the movement and the flexibility of their body.

This is the aesthetic and spiritual message that I attempt to transmit to my students, instructors and whomsoever chooses me as their guide into the magic world of freediving. This together with the message of Jacques 'the Amphibian:' enjoy yourself, and try to make each dive a better experience than the last; forget about your origins as a bipedal terrestrial and give yourself over to the laws of the sea; listen to the dolphin. No one can teach you better than a dolphin.

Ah, I'm forgetting a detail... In all of this I was somehow able to make a family!

In 2002, during one of my freediving courses, I met an incredible girl called Irene. She knew very little about freediving, but this was to be expected since she was more bird than dolphin! Irene was an acrobatic pilot, and champion of Europe and the world. They say that opposites attract, and so three years later she became my wife, and then... mother to my three sons: Tommaso, Niccolò and Giulio.

The ocean inside us

WATER IMITATES LIFE
AND LIFE IS NOTHING BUT WATER

Stewart M. Brooks

Man's acquatic nature

The similarity between man and the sea is incredible, both from a physiological and chemical point of view. Our bodies are composed primarily of water: in an adult this is around 60% of total mass, while in babies it is 80%, and in the human embryo as much as 97%. As Jacques Mayol used to say, there's a genuine ocean inside every one of us.

There is an extraordinary affinity between human blood and seawater. In fact, from a chemical point of view, the sea is very similar to all of the internal liquids of the animals and vegetables that populate it, so much so that it could be called the 'external blood' or 'lymph' of these organisms. The plasma of human blood has a salinity very close to what the sea is believed to have had in past eras, when animal life started to emerge from the seas to populate the land. To this day however blood contains a high concentration of sodium chloride, otherwise known as regular table salt.

The analogies don't finish here. Blood nourishes all of the tissues of the body through the transport of oxygen and proteins indispensable for respiration and the nutrition of cells. In a certain sense the sea acts in the same way, carrying the plankton that form the base of the marine food chain. Just like blood, the sea has a respiratory function: almost all marine animals depend on oxygen dissolved in the water in order to breathe. Doctor Brooks wrote: "Life, which was born in the seas, was unable to survive on land until the moment in which the forces of evolution created an organism capable of bringing with it a little piece of the sea." On emerging from the seas life distinguished itself from the sea, but all the while kept within itself a small piece of its origin. In his deepest genetic memory, man still possesses a relic of his aquatic past.

If this is true for the adult human, then what can we say about the newborn baby who has just finished spending nine months in a liquid habitat? The foetus grows in the womb, fed and completely enveloped in amniotic fluid – in this phase it is as good as living in water. Its lungs are 'short circuited:' they exist but are not yet 'online,' and will only start functioning after birth, as a reflex to the umbilical chord being cut. The oxygen required by the millions of tiny cells that constitute the foetus is supplied by blood circulation, nourished by the placenta through the umbilical chord. The placenta is a kind of 'second mother', an intermediary between the baby and the mother. In the final weeks of gestation the foetus begins to practice the breathing reflex, inhaling amniotic fluid. Another impressive amphibious characteristic of the human foetus is to be found in its heart. During the nine months of intrauterine life the cardiac muscle evolves by transforming from a heart with two cavities, like that of a fish, to three cavities, as of a reptile, and finally to the four cavities that defines a mammalian heart.

It's easy to imagine the intimate relationship and the strong bonds between the neonate and the liquid element – the 'primordial broth' from which we departed. This is the reason why newborn babies immersed in water don't find it completely unpleasant. The newborn baby finds itself with joy in the universal liquid that it already knows, and which protected it during its prenatal life in the amniotic sack of its mother's womb.

There is one more aquatic quality of man connected to the early days of life: in its first three months the newborn baby's haemoglobin has a greater affinity with oxygen than an adult's, but after three months this feature tends to gradually diminish. This means that even from a physiological perspective a baby is more adapted to apnea in its first hundred days of life.

Underwater birth has been practiced with remarkable success for years in many countries. It has come to be considered a modern technique, although in many 'primitive' cultures the act of submerging women in water during the difficult moments of labour and childbirth is a practice derived from the most ancient tradition. Some examples are the pygmy populations that live in the forest bordering the Ituri River in Congo, any tribe that occupies the Peruvian part of the Amazon forest, and the aborigines of the western coast of Australia. Some cases of water births were documented also in the ancient Maori popu-

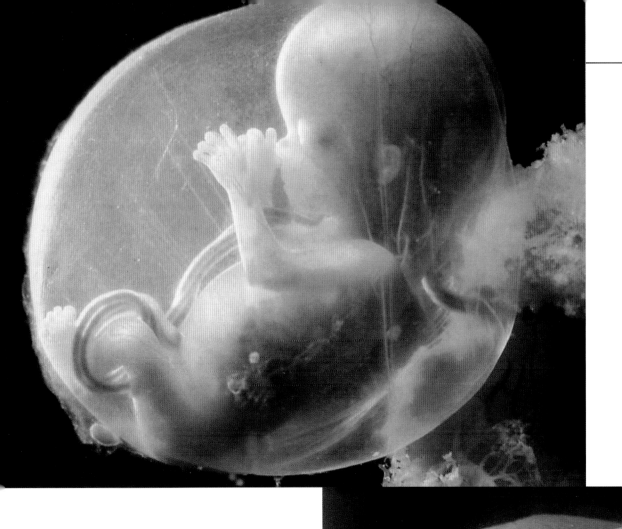

These images show the human embryo completely
immersed in liquid, and demonstrate the deep affinity that
man has with water.
It is easy to imagine the intimate relationship and the strong
connection between the newborn and the liquid element –
the 'primordial broth' from which it departed. This is why,
if a newborn baby is immersed in water, it doesn't find itself
too much out of its comfort zone.

lation of New Zealand, and the Indians of the Panama. This method avoids the trauma of an abrupt passage from the familiar liquid universe of the mother's belly to the dry and completely unknown universe of terrestrial life.

A very complex investigation was carried out, conducted with a psychoanalytical method on a sample population of children from four to ten years of age, all born underwater. It was discovered that the percentage of individuals who were distinctly extroverted, communicative, optimists was about 70% higher than the percentage amongst contemporaries born with normal dry childbirth. According to psychologists and doctors this can be explained by the

fact that the first force experienced by the new-born is not gravitational – violent and towards the ground – but that of water: sweet, homogenous and upward. We can guess at the reason why this happens, but not the precise way in which these psychological changes come about. This is one of the enigmas and unknowns related to the mysterious link between man and the water.

Stathis Haggi wasn't able to hold his breath for even a minute in 'dry' static apnea. He didn't know why it happened, but he knew that underwater everything was made easy. Situations like this have been seen often, and confirmed by all the top freedivers of the last thirty years – even today most athletes are able

to achieve better results in the water than in open air. I can even confirm this myself. During medical tests conducted in laboratories I was able to hold my breath only one time, and with great difficulty, for more than five minutes. In the water however, when I am in peak fitness I can complete training tables that include, for example, ten repetitions of six minute static apneas, with one minute recovery between them, or fifteen five-minute breath holds with forty five seconds recovery, or twenty five three-minute breath holds with fifteen seconds recovery. Doctors told me that I could only be completely relaxed in the water, while in air even the most relaxed position would involve some contracted muscles. This explanation didn't convince me entirely: how is it possible that such a minor detail as a slight muscular contraction of a few small muscles could cut my performance by such a margin? The solution needs to be studied in the liquid element. When I am completely immersed in water, there are extraordinary phenomena that have both physical and mental repercussions. The water becomes something magical: I know I am a human being, and that I need to breathe, but I don't feel any kind of compulsion to do so.

Professor Luigi Odone lecturer of clinical psychology at the University of Genoa, was occupied for years with the psychodynamic features and the psychological profile of the freediver. He maintained that in apnea underwater man returns to his origins, since during prenatal life he has expected an aquatic existence, and he never completely forgets this expectation. Man's unconscious mind definitely knows a thing or two about his origins and his relationship with nature, the elements and the universe…

We are born marine animals, whether in the ontogenetic sense (birth of an individual) or phylogenetic sense (birth of a species). According to professor Odone, the process of psychological development in man is nothing but a summary of the preceding process of developmental biology. More than a level of memory, it brings a level of intuition: where the memory fails to reach consciously we succeed with the unconscious mind. In the moment we dive beneath the surface, we apply what can be called a 'deep regression' – a capacity to return the psyche to a state of calm. In water we joyously reclaim that dimension of relief from tension, of comfortable security, and of the peace that we knew in the womb – a return to Eden. Birth involves a dynamic biology, a force towards life and the struggle to survive (to cry, to move, and to chew mum's nipples…). From the moment a child is born there is an end to the homeostasis, as Freud calls it – the equilibrium without any driving force that has defined the first nine months of life. Only in an aquatic environment do our minds succeed in reaching harmony with the archetypal sensations of peace and happiness.

The two worlds, one above and one below water, can be seen as 'parallels without connection.' This explains why we can only achieve impressive performances while we are immersed in the liquid element. Professor Odone claimed that it would be very difficult to explain this phenomenon in scientific terms; we must simply accept it, grounding it on intuitive understanding and senses.

Children are particularly attracted to water and the marine environment: perhaps for curiosity, perhaps out of a desire to discover a new and unknown world, or maybe even because it reminds them of the aquatic dimension that defined their prenatal existence. Teaching children with aquatic activities is a great help, both from a physical and mental perspective, and helps them to develop a healthy bond with both themselves and the environment.

I'm able to reach
good performances
in apnea only if
I'm completely
submerged in the
water. It could be that
only in this condition
of total physical and
mental relaxation
am I able to return
to the peace and
calm reminiscent of
prenatal life.

Apnea: science and science fiction

In the fifties the French doctor of physiology Cabarrou stated categorically that man would be unable to freedive past the depth of fifty meters: "Après, il s'ecrase!" he declared ("Any deeper and you will be crushed!") Almost a decade passed before the truth and the courage of a man could prove him wrong.

Raimondo Bucher set the first freediving world record in 1949, descending to 30 meters where he handed over a parchment enclosed in a watertight container to an incredulous hard hat diver. After Raimondo many others went deeper, but no one had reached the fateful depth of 50 meters that Cabarrou had defined as the insurmountable limit of man. That was until Enzo Maiorca decided to snub the theories, and in the glorious year of 1961 he crossed for the first time that portentous depth, at which he would supposedly be flattened by the terrible pressure.

Doctor Cabarrou had based his ominous prophecy of the crushing future of apnea past 50 meters by using several hypothetical containers that were supposed to resemble the human thoracic cage in its composition and resilience to hydrostatic pressure. The thoracic cage is of course not just a static container containing the heart and lungs; it is also the packaging of a complex physiological mechanism that responds to precise rules.

Ten years later we had the reply to the innumerable questions triggered by Maiorca's dive. Initially it was argued that the feat could be explained by 'hereditary factors' and progressive training, but the true explanation has since been identified as bradycardia and the 'blood shift.'

In 1974, at Elba, Jacques Mayol underwent a very delicate medical test that consisted in having a blood sample taken during a dive. A catheter was introduced into his elbow, in the vena cava superior (apparently extremely uncomfortable for Mayol), and this allowed doctors to measure the venal intrathoracic blood pressure at depths of 40 and 60 meters. They noticed that the quantity of blood contained in the thorax during the dive increased from 1.0 up to 2.2 litres. This demonstrated the drawing of blood into the thorax; the so-called 'blood shift' hypothesized for the first time in 1968 by Karl Shaefer, a physiologist in the US Navy. It is the blood shift that negates the theory of Cabarrou. This physiological mechanism is manifested in all apnea dives beyond a certain depth, and can be explained very easily. At sea level there is one atmosphere of pressure, given by the weight of about 10 kilometers of air above us. Descending under the sea we experience an additional atmosphere of pressure for every ten meters of depth, so there are two atmospheres at 10 meters, three atmospheres at 20 meters, six at 50 meters and eleven at 100 meters. This pressure acts on all the air cavities contained in our body, which of course include the lungs. The air contained in the lungs is reduced in volume according to Boyle's law, which states that at a constant temperature the pressure and volume of a gas are inversely proportional to each other.

So at 100 meters for example, the air contained in the lungs will occupy an eleventh of its initial volume: our lungs are therefore eleven times smaller than they were on the surface. The space left over by this reduction in size of the lungs can't be left as a vacuum, otherwise we really would risk Cabarrou's 'implosion' – a collapse of the thorax due to the external pressure of the water (which at 100 meters is equal to eleven kilograms on each square centimeter of our body). The fact that this doesn't happen is thanks to the blood shift: the blood is drawn back from the periphery of the body, where

This German engraving from 1555 shows a 'Subaquatic Attacker' who swims with the use of an inflatable ring similar to that designed by Leonardo da Vinci. There is evidence of subacquatic activity in even more ancient times.

sponds to hydrostatic pressure, but it is also an active mechanism that allows for a more prudent usage of oxygen by the important organs only, such as the brain and heart, instead of the less important peripheral tissues.

Dolphins (which of all the marine mammals are the closest relative to humans) and other cetaceans habitually reach depths of great magnitude. The sperm whale and the elephant seal are the undisputed champions of depth, capable of descending to well over a thousand meters. When the sperm whale dives it stores about three thousand litres of air in its lungs, equivalent to a twenty-litre scuba bottle filled to 150 atmospheres. At 1,000 meters, where the pressure is 101 atmospheres, the volume of gas contained in its lungs will have reduced to about one hundredth, or thirty litres. At this point the sperm whale should 'implode' – its immense body should collapse inwards, being crushed to pieces. Obviously this doesn't happen – in fact at this depth the animal even has the strength to engage in furious struggles with the giant squid, its dish of choice. This is only possible because the whale's body has made in-

(left)
A print depicting the first autonomous dive suit by Roqueiroland Denayrouse (France 1865). Man has always been attracted to the sea, but only in the last sixty years has he started to use mechanical apparatuses that allow him to continue to breathe at great depth.

(below)
The drive towards the conquest of the abyss was born mainly from a desire to exploit the riches of the sea. Nowadays man has descended, breathing special mixes of hydrogen, helium and oxygen, to the abyssal depth of 330 meters.

there are no organs critical to survival, and into the lungs, where it fills the space left empty by the reduction in volume of the air in the lungs. Since blood is a liquid, and liquids are incompressible, this mechanism saves us from implosion.

During a freedive I very clearly feel the onset of the blood shift, normally just after the depth of 60 meters: it feels like all of a sudden there is more air in my lungs and I have less urge to breathe. Many doctors maintain however that the phenomenon of the blood shift, which today allows us to reach depths that not so long ago were considered inconceivable, may one day create a physiological limit to man's freediving potential. This is because at ever greater depths the heart could become 'engulfed' by the high quantity of blood returning from the periphery, and find it impossible to continue beating. This is of course all conjecture, especially considering all the contradictions and wrong turns that hyperbaric medicine has taken in the sixty-year history of freediving. Furthermore the blood shift is not an entirely passive phenomenon that only re-

Modern medicine has often deliberately ignored psychological factors in a vain attempt to mechanistically explain certain physiological phenomena. In freediving the power of the mind can enable us to reach results that are inexplicable by modern science.

credible adaptations to the (essentially hostile) environment in which it lives and moves. As well as collapsible lungs, seals, whales and dolphins also have collapsible tracheas and bronchi, due to the fact that the cartilage they are constructed from is not rigid, as it is in humans. Furthermore they have supple ribs, which are not attached to the sternum, and are therefore more flexible under compression. But it is most importantly the cardiovascular system which makes such incredible dives possible for these creatures: the blood that irrigates the periphery

(as well as the fins, which are just hands and feet rudimentarily transformed into swimming paddles) is sucked back into the thorax; heart rate decreases significantly and this greatly reduces oxygen consumption.

The seal, which is more comparable to a human being, is able to dive to 300 meters, and can slow it's heart rate almost instantaneously from one hundred and twenty down to twenty beats per minute. This is called bradycardia, and is seen as a very important phenomenon by all freediving researchers.

When holding my breath motionless in the water I feel my heart rate slow gradually down to thirty beats per minute. The effect is much more pronounced in a deep dive. I've often stopped on the bottom, at the end of a descent to over 100 meters, and concentrated exclusively on my heart. Even though it seems unbelievable I feel my heart beat only once every seven or eight seconds. The doctors in my team smile when I tell them about this impression, and say that it's impossible for a man's heart rate to slow to eight beats a minute. We shall see. I am convinced that as soon as they are able to make a Holter monitor (the instrument used to record an electrocardiogram) waterproof to over 100 meters, then this phenomenon will be verified also. Slowing of the heart rate isn't restricted to sea mammals only, and can be seen in all other warm-blooded animals with lungs: not just beavers and hippopotamuses (which are to be expected, given their habitat), but even such animals as dogs, if they are forced to keep their head underwater, experience a clear slowing of the heart. It has even been seen in ducks (which are of course birds, not mammals), and was called the 'dive reflex' or 'washbasin reflex', since you only need to dunk the face in a bowl of water to stimulate an automatic reduction of heart rate. The dive reflex is an instinctive reaction, fully developed even in newborn babies and the smallest children who, though they may be unable to swim yet, will still instinctively hold their breath if submerged in a pool.

The reflex can be nullified through the use of specific drugs, and experiments have been done with seals that caused them to interrupt a dive and ascend to the surface with obvious signs of difficulty. The dive reflex explains why tests done with dry apneas or breath holds in a hyperbaric chamber have always given different results to tests done with apnea in the water. In my case, the difficulty I have in performing a certain time in dry apnea is far greater than for the same length of time in water. This is also caused by the fact that only in water are we able to reach complete physical relaxation and mental concentration. In fact there are automatic physical advantages: as well as the bradycardia we described earlier there is a reduction in blood pressure and a general muscular decontraction. It's almost as if my body knows that any time it is submerged in water it has to get ready to hold its breath, and these reflexes become more and more enhanced with training.

Another interesting parameter is the production of carbon dioxide. The percentage of carbon dioxide found by gas analysis of exhaled air can vary greatly depending on the type of apnea. After a dry static apnea the concentration of carbon dioxide increases, following predicted values, but after the same length of apnea in a swimming pool the concentration

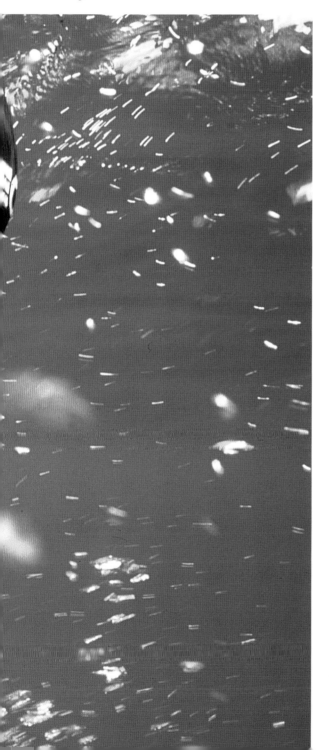

stays the same, and after a deep dive it even drops!

There has been much progress on the road to scientific understanding of the human body in apnea, but there are still many doubts and unexplained physiological phenomena. Doctor Luca Torcello, who has followed me since I started taking my first steps in freediving, has conducted countless medical tests on me during my training. In an interview several years ago he confessed quite sincerely and disarmingly that at the start of every set of tests he would set off in the direction of research, with the hope of giving an answer to existing questions, but at the end of each test numerous mysteries remained unsolved and, moreover,

new problems and questions had emerged. According to him we are only at the beginning of a mysterious and fascinating path: we know neither its direction nor its destination, but we must walk it all the same. However it will take time, a lot of time.

I have often been asked if I feel like a laboratory rat, and I have always replied in the negative. I dive for myself, for the pleasure of going down underwater, and the emotions that I experience there: I don't dive for medicine. However if my experiences and the fact that I have been submitted to extreme conditions is of interest to medical science then I think that it's important I make myself available for it.

In my humble opinion, hyperbaric medicine often has an inappropriate approach to the study of freediving: the current trend is to identify the laws (departing from purely theoretical principles) that govern the way man's body responds to apnea, and to presume that they are applicable to any subject. This isn't the way forward. Any individual freediver, when subjected to extreme stimuli, may respond physiologically in a unique and unpredictable way. In order to halve the atmospheric pressure found at sea level we need to climb a five thousand meter mountain, but to double it we need only dive 10 meters beneath the sea. This gives an idea of how much more conditions vary in water than in air, and of how extreme conditions are beyond 100 meters depth. How can we assume that everyone who lives and breathes in one atmosphere of pressure if subjected to such extreme variations would all react in the same way?

And speaking of limits, what depth is a human being capable of?

Normally one might think that the depth limit of man would be determined by the duration of the dive, but it isn't necessarily so. I descended to 150 meters and returned in three minutes (and I wasn't exactly in a rush: I spent about 10 seconds on the bottom to greet my two safety divers, and at about 60 meters from the surface I let go of the lift bag in order to finish my ascent slowly pulling on the line). A dive in which you descend with a weighted sled and return to the surface with an inflated lift bag could be considered a static apnea, since

In a deep freedive the human body undergoes unimaginable stress. In response it triggers survival reflexes similar to those used by the sea mammals: powerful bradycardia (the heart slows down to seven to ten beats per minute), contraction of the spleen, and reduction in lung volume. All of this allows us to return to the surface in one piece.

it doesn't require any physical force. My best times in static are close to eight minutes, so if the result of a dive was indeed determined by dive time then I would be able to freedive to 400 meters! Unfortunately this isn't the case: the real problem is the ability to equalise the middle ear.

(above and above on the next page) There have been many interesting tests done in hyperbaric chambers on the physiology of man at high ambient pressures. The biggest problem however is that the freediver's body isn't submerged in water, and so you cannot reproduce the same phenomena that exist in a deep freedive. In dry air everything is more difficult and less natural. However in a hyperbaric chamber, after having breathed pure oxygen, there have been breath holds performed of almost thirty minutes.

As depth increases so does the pressure on the ear drum, causing it to flex inwards. At this point we must equalise, taking air from the lungs and directing it towards the middle ear to force the eardrum back to its normal position. If we don't equalise then the ear drum will rupture. This is what gives us the real limitation that makes deep freediving so difficult: at 150 meters lung volume is one sixteenth of initial volume, making it almost impossible to access any air in your lungs in order to send to the ears. The solution to the problem is in the reduction of equalisation frequency, so that you can effect the last equalisation at a greater depth. On Mayol's advice I also tried a new and extremely difficult equalisation technique. It consists in removing my nose plug at 80 meters and completely flooding the airways. If there's water then there can't be any air, and saving the air in this way should allow me to reach a greater depth. This technique is especially complicated and practiced only at the highest level. Another new technique is called the 'mouth fill.' In this type of equalisation the mouth is completely filled with air at the greatest depth possible. The epiglottis is then closed (to pre-

vent the air from returning to the lungs) and the soft palate can be opened to allow the air access to the Eustachian tubes. Then the jaw, cheeks and lastly the tongue are used to progressively push air into the Eustachian tubes, ensuring an equalised pressure on the eardrum.

I am convinced, as are my colleagues, that within a few years the barrier of 300 meters will be broken using these kind of equalisation techniques. And medicine pushes us even further: after having for so many years imposed limits on man's potential in freediving – which were punctually disproved – it now seems to have changed tack. Some research groups sustain that if man continues to adapt physically and mentally as he has done so far, in the future we will be able to surpass the unreal depth of 350 meters.

The prospect of breathing underwater without limit to time or depth has been investigated with different concepts of surgery: the idea is to find a solution using very advanced technology (especially in the materials used) to construct an absolutely revolutionary breathing apparatus – no less than artificial gills. In fish and other animals that 'breathe' the water, the gills perform a function very similar to the lungs of animals that breathe the air: they fill with water just as lungs fill with air, supply the blood with the oxygen necessary for the function of the animal, and simultaneously eliminate substances (in particular inert gases) that are damaging or unnecessary. Artificial gills would be nothing more than devices that exchange gases by diffusion through a semipermeable membrane that separates the immersed animal and the water that surrounds it. The *Great Encylopedia of the Sea* states that Doctor Robb was the first to prove, in 1965, that mammals can exchange sufficient quantities of gas with an aqueous environment by diffusion across thin artificial films. He was able to keep hamsters alive in a closed container that had walls made of silicon and was completely immersed in water that was kept oxygenated by the emission of gas bubbles. The oxygen consumed by the hamsters reduced the partial pressure of this gas in the chamber, and since the concentration of oxygen in the water around the container was kept very high, the oxygen diffused into the container at a rate determined by the metabolism of the hamster. Carbon dioxide produced by the animal increased the partial pressure of this gas inside the container, and since the partial pressure of carbon dioxide in the surrounding water was minimal, the toxic gas diffused out through the membrane. Two years later, in 1967, Paganelli, Bateman and Rahn analysed the passage of gas through a similar system, using a Millipore instead of silicon rubber. Millipore membranes are used to separate a liquid from a gas. If the pores are small enough then the surface of the material will be able to withstand very high hydrostatic pressures: for example water will not be able to penetrate an air-filled container submerged in water if the walls of the container are made from a hydrophobic (water-repellent) Millipore membrane. A very basic example of a Millipore membrane

(below)
The hyperbaric chamber on board the Anfitrite. The team is composed of two deep divers who can operate at up to 300 meters. These are the guardian angels of my guardian angels. If I have a problem, my divers intervene, but if my divers have a problem then these guys intervene.

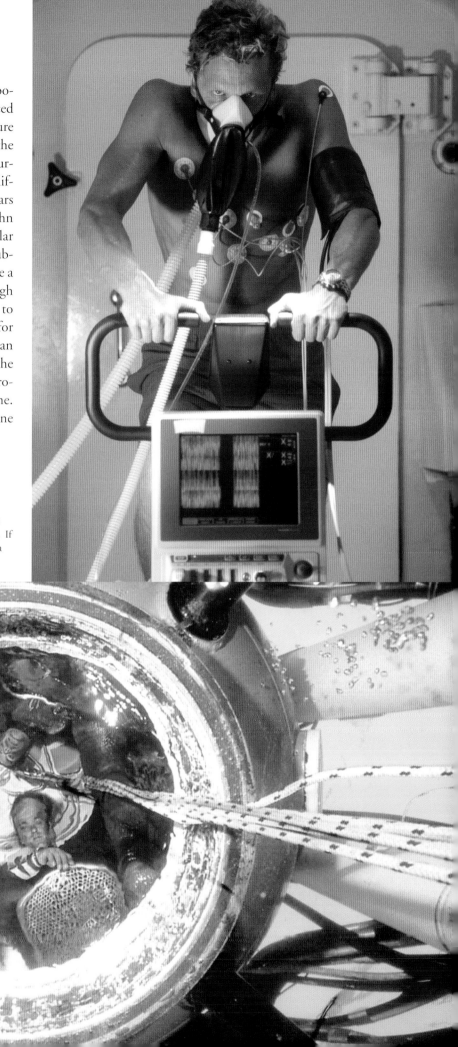

is any kind of wet cloth: a bubble of air underneath the material is trapped by surface tension, which stops it from escaping through the pores (in fact a normal scarf can be transformed into a life preserver to help save a drowning swimmer). But back to the experiment. Based on careful measurement of the flow of gas at varying speeds of water flow over the membrane, this system allowed the researchers to predict that it would be possible for a resting man to stay submerged indefinitely in a river, if he was inside a closed air space with Millipore membranes covering eight square meters of its surface, and if the river maintained a constant speed of water flow over the membrane of nine kilometers per hour. In these conditions the total pressure inside the chamber would be less than the exterior, but the partial pressure of oxygen inside the air space would be stable at 100mmHg. The elimination of carbon dioxide from the air inside the closed chamber wouldn't be a problem, since carbon dioxide is much more soluble than oxygen, and would easily diffuse into the surrounding fluid.

A practical application of a similar underwater survival system could be a kind of rigid case diver – the precursor to the hard hat diver, where the diver worked inside a big bottomless box placed on the seafloor, and the pressure of air introduced through a hose expelled water from the box. But instead of being in a dry hyperbaric case the subject would be immersed in a hypobaric chamber: a diver with wetsuit, mask and fins, who has no need for a scuba tank since he can get the oxygen directly from the water by means of the breathable walls of his chamber being exposed to a violent current.

At the same time in 1966 an American bioengineer called Ayres had created a different design for artificial gills, with the idea of reconditioning exhaled air by diffusion into seawater: in effect a rebreather that looks like a car radiator, consisting of pairs of membranes with an area of 116 square centimeters and 1/25 of a millimeter thick and built-in tubes with a diameter of 16 millimeters. Forty eight 30-centimeter sections of such tubing gave Ayres 20 square meters of permeable membrane exposed to the water. However in order to make it work the diver would have to move forwards contin-

big as a vacuum cleaner and two tubes sticking out of his chest), the heart muscle must remain functional, the lungs must be excluded from circulation and the artificial gills would have to be connected to the main pulmonary artery. At this point the surgical operation would become irreversible, and the diver would be forced to live underwater for the rest of their life. We would have created a new human race, but at the same time we would have produced many physiological problems that would be extremely difficult to resolve: dispersion of body heat, waterlogged skin and tissue, and not least the fact that carbon dioxide is twenty times more water-soluble than oxygen, and passes five times easier through the silicon membrane: a diver who must maintain a partial pressure of oxygen in the arteries of 100mmHg would have to have a partial pressure of carbon dioxide less than 100mmHg, and this is less than what the human body requires to function. These physiological and chemical obstacles are similar to an organ rejection after a transplant: technically it is possible to substitute the heart, lungs and kidneys, but the human body isn't accustomed to this kind of surgical violence, and responds by expelling the foreign organs. So although it's technically possible with modern surgery to make an incision underneath the left armpit of a hypothetical amphibian man and connect an artery and a vein to a small machine that would eliminate carbon dioxide and replenish oxygen (to a percentage that would depend on the operating depth), it is still impossible in

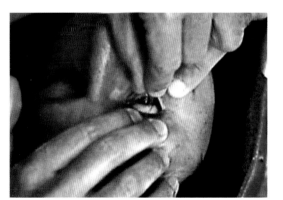

practice to overcome the physical and chemical hurdles related to the partial pressures of the inert gases. Similarly, it is technically possible to 'short circuit' the lungs, introducing a flour-

uously, a bit like some sharks whose gills don't have mobile opercula like other fish, and who therefore have to swim incessantly. Then there would be numerous other problems presented by the different levels of solubility in water of gases exposed to pressure. This unavoidable problem would be present even if we had artificial gills that worked just like a fish's, i.e. if they were irrigated with blood that absorbed the oxygen directly from the surrounding water. In short the physiological and technological understanding required to create such an apparatus are within reach of bioengineers and doctors. However apart from the difficulty involved in miniaturising a device as complex as the heart-lung system (think about the artificial heart, which allows a patient awaiting a transplant to move around with a machine as

Through training my body adapts gradually to the water and everything that it entails. It's almost as if my body knows that every time it is submerged in the water it has to make itself ready for apnea. This is what enabled me to dive to 150 meters.

Application of the special contact lenses. Over the years the freediver's equipment has changed completely. It is impossible to dive to current world record depths with conventional masks: one either uses lenses or dives with bare eyes.

carbon compound into the respiratory system that would fill up the alveoli, bronchi and trachea. A man who had been treated in this way would breathe through the machine under his armpit, with the thorax completely immobile, and without diaphragmatic contractions to alert him to a drop in oxygen or a rise in carbon dioxide. It would be a paradoxical leap backwards in time, even if it was a voluntary step. Being able to breathe directly from the water instead of from the surrounding air would be a kind of return to the embryonic state, when the baby is connected to the mother via its umbilical chord, receiving oxygen directly into its blood. It would be the ideal solution for any problems of decompression, but as we

have seen it would require that the volunteers completely renounce their natural terrestrial state. Unthinkable? Who knows. If in the future our descendents must make do with what they have, or if the earth has been so altered that it can only be inhabited by physiologically different creatures, or if man has travelled to remote worlds that can only be explored and

In recent years the number of elite freedivers has increased dramatically. This has afforded researchers a greater number of subjects for their studies. However it has been shown that two freedivers can respond completely differently to the same stimulus.

According to some theories there are many adaptations and physiological mechanisms that are triggered during a freediving descent the moment the light level is decreased to below a certain value, independently of the depth reached.

colonised by completely reconditioned people, then the hypothesis of the man-fish might be taken into serious consideration, and perhaps put into practice.

Jacques Piccard, the famous Swiss physicist and son of the creator of *Trieste* (the bathysphere that touched a record depth of 10,912 meters at the bottom of Mariana's Trench), asked the same question in a beautiful essay on the evolution of human activity in the seas: "When we think about the divers of ancient times, the underwater soldiers who according to legend were able to resupply besieged cities, Alexander the Great who in the middle ages supposedly descended to great depths in a glass sphere, the men and women who dove for pearls, corals or cannonballs, the first uncertain steps of the 17th century, the dawn of underwater technology in the 18th century, the workmen of the sea in the 19th century, and the grand conquests of our century, we realise that the history of diving has certainly had a beginning and an evolution that has

been aided by the technologies that man has developed, but most importantly we realise that above and beyond this technology there is the unbridled passion of man for everything that isn't human: children pretend they are monkeys climbing a tree, while adults imitate the eagles, flying in hang gliders, and others emulate fish, diving underneath the water. And when technology no longer suffices we invent Alice in Wonderland, who is small enough to live with mice, or Gulliver, who is big enough to conquer the world. Science fiction precedes its realisation, and if we go back to the time of Welles and imagine flying saucers and space flight, then whether we are children or adults, workers or scholars, Buddhist monks or electronic engineers, we experience an almost permanent fiction that conducts us from myth to reality, towards a world whose control seems to escape us from one moment to the next. Will we one day find ourselves swimming free of any impediment, and at any depth of the ocean?"

The latest research in hyperbaric medicine has established that man should be physiologically capable of reaching a depth of 300 meters. They have calculated that this is the depth at which the maximum limit in gas compression of air in the lungs would be reached, and beyond this depth the walls of the lungs would collapse, causing irreparable damage. Sea mammals can go a lot deeper because they have a different anatomical make-up.

A challenge
beyond limits

LIFE IS A SHIVER THAT LEAVES AS QUICKLY AS IT
COMES — IT'S ALL A BALANCE OVER THE MADNESS

Vasco Rossi

The last breath before I confront the abyss. At depth the environment around me is unique. Light gives way to obscurity, the force of gravity is muted, the silence is absolute and interrupted only by a heartbeat that pervades me completely. At depth my body is profoundly altered: my lungs are the size of apples, my heart rate is at seven or eight beats a minute, and blood pressure is enormous. Despite all this I feel only pleasure. It is a dive into the soul, and each time coming back is a choice I have to make.

Why the extremes

Holding the breath is one of the most unnatural things a man can do. We can go several weeks without eating, and days without drinking, but no more than a few minutes without breathing. We might ask ourselves why someone would be drawn to such a tough and difficult discipline: how can one find pleasure and stimulus in an activity that is essentially a sufferance? In reality freediving is a gradual rediscovery of oneself, a journey inside, which, if it's done right, can completely nullify the painful aspect that goes with holding the breath, and even open the door to beautiful sensations and emotions.

To get to this point requires time and patience, and it will only occur when you learn how to freedive with the mind rather than with the body – with willpower rather than muscular power. "How are you able to dive so deep? What's your secret?" are the most common questions that aspiring freedivers put to

me. As always I punctually disappoint them by saying: "My secret is that I have understood that there are no secrets." There are no magic potions, only training. And a lot of it. Not just physically, but (more importantly) mentally.

In daily training physical preparation is of great importance. Jacques Mayol was the first to introduce the practice of yoga to deep freediving. He was the one who taught me *pranayama* (the branch of yoga that deals with the dynamics of breathing), diaphragmatic respiration, and techniques of relaxation and autosuggestion. Every one of us has a gift from nature, a biological adaptation that allows us to achieve certain results underwater: diving to certain depths, and holding the breath for certain periods of time. With physical training we can improve on this, but only to a certain unsurpassable point: and this is what constitutes the physical limit of each one of us. To go beyond that we must have the right mental preparation, and so techniques of mental and physical relaxation are indispensable. The emotional factor is the most dominant in freediving. Before I attempt a deep freedive I must find the concentration and motivation to do so inside of me, within my psyche and will-force. It is important to always have an incentive, and after you have set a record it is normal to have some kind of internal satisfaction. We must however react to this tendency to relax, by always looking for new motivation.

If it is cold outside and there is a strong north wind blowing then obviously the last thing that you're going to want to do is throw yourself in the sea for a couple of hours. It would be a lot more comfortable to stay at home on the couch, watching a film together with friends. But if you think that in that same exact moment your rival who you have just beaten is in training to surpass you then you forget about everything and get out the door. This is the winning attitude, and my trainer Massimo Giudicelli was successful in passing it on to me. He insisted that the spirit of sacrifice and the ability to support hard work were the most important characteristics of an athlete, if he or she wanted to perform

at a high level. I hadn't known Massimo for long when one day, after a long training session that had left me terribly cold and anxious to get home and take off my wetsuit, he looked at me and said: "You have to get used to these small sacrifices. How can you hope to bear the discomfort and pressure of deep freediving when you can't even put up with a cold wetsuit?" His little lectures were often genuine lessons of life, that helped me to mature both as man and sportsman. Even more than a friend, he was my psychologist. One time, just after a world record, he warned me: "Enjoy this victory – you've earned it. But from tomorrow start looking ahead. What's happened today is forgotten tomorrow. You would do well to leave it behind also, and start off again on a new adventure. Don't think that you're a champion, that you've gotten to the end: you have to convince yourself that you're a nobody. That way, when you get back in the water you'll still have the enthusiasm and euphoria of a kid in search of victory. If you happen to finish second then may it be because someone is a stronger diver than you, and never because you haven't tried your hardest."

In freediving there are contrasting situations: the hard sacrifices and intense effort during the phases of physical training, and on the other hand the pleasure and emotions of swimming with the dolphins or a freedive down the side of a coral wall. Determination is the desire to beat a rival, contrasted with a rivalry with oneself. Competition and the apparent absence of competitiveness. Humility and presumption. Relaxation and determination. Joy, excitement and light heartedness, but also unsparing tenacity and implacable resolve. All this is freediving.

I dive into the abyss to see how deep 'my sea' is, and I freedive in order to enjoy emotions and sensations which would otherwise be inaccessible. I don't know what it is that pushes me down there, and I'm not even that interested in finding out – the beautiful thing is that I will continue doing it as long as my body allows. This is how I reply to anyone who asks me why I keep on trying to go deeper. The commitment is tremendous and ab-

solute, not only for the physical risks that are associated (and there are many), but also for the determination that is required. It is both a mental and existential determination: to live in order to go beyond the limits of life. It is even more than an ideal, and there are many other men and women who possess this absolute determination. Some of them display it by skiing down walls of ice, trusting their lives on the millimeter-thick blades of their skis; a different type of diver throw themselves off the tops of cliffs and skim past rock walls before opening their parachutes at the last moment; other adventurers steer down raging rivers in a tiny canoe; others climb smooth and sheer cliff faces with their bare hands; and still others cross oceans in rowboats or even swimming! There are many 'No Limits' men and women, operating in different environments and with different techniques. However all of them have the same stimulus, the same attraction to the extreme, and the need to go beyond limits. What is it that causes this? What drives the alpinists, explorers and divers to attempt that which no man has done before?

Israeli and American scientists have discovered a connection between DNA and the spirit of adventure. With poetic license this common element was called the "The Ulysses Factor." According to these researchers it is mainly caused by dopamine, the substance that allows neurons in the brain to 'speak' to each other. We all have it, but it seems we don't all use it in the same way. The Israeli scientists came to the conclusion that 15% of the population is able to use it better than the rest. Why? The answer is in the structure of the gene which codes for the protein that couples with dopamine. This protein 'sniffs out' dopamine and chemically reacts with it in order to 'refuel' the neuron: we all need this 'fuel' but while most of us produce 'regular' petrol, there is a group of 15% who produce 'high-octane.'

This dopamine receptor is also amplified by anyone who uses the drug cocaine. So it seems that a genetic feature allows some individuals to have a kind of natural high, which unlike an illicit drug, doesn't leave any traces

in urine or get you in trouble with the authorities! But what is it exactly?

In order to find out a team of scientists from Jerusalem subjected a group of one hundred and twenty volunteers (staff and students of the University of Ben Gurion) to a double-sided kind of test: both psychological and genetic. The subjects had to respond to one hundred questions regarding their personality – here are some of them: "Do you feel like everything will always be alright, even in situations where others are worried? Do you always look for new experiences, even when others think they might be a waste of time? Do you do things your way, without worrying about how others might like them done? Do you feel tense and worried when you have to do something that you haven't done before? When nothing is happening in your life do you try to find something new and exciting?"

"Taken by themselves these questions might seem simplistic," was a comment made by Richard Ebstein, the head of the research, "But if the subjects are honest it will allow us to identify the thrill-seekers: persons who love novelty and have an adventurous character."

The scores ranged from five or six (for those who consider leaving their house in the evening a risky venture), to twenty five (those who believe in the motto "I want to try everything once before I die").

"We took a blood sample from each of the volunteers in order to extract their DNA," continues Ebstein, "and in 15% of these we found a particular structure in the gene that codes for the protein that attaches to dopamine. So we concentrated on this group, and when we studied the results of their questionnaires we found that they had an average score of eighteen, against an average of fifteen in the entire group of volunteers." These results were confirmed by a study conducted in the Washington, United States by the National Institute of Health. What does it all mean? That, according to the Israeli scientist, "For the first time we have identified a connection between a particular genetic makeup and the spirit of adventure."

Mayol often told me: "If you feel good then keep going. It's not just the physical aspect that matters – if anything the mental aspect, which has confounded scientific research, is even more important." These secrets are known only to 'my sea' and I.

(on the next page)
My preparation begins about ten months before a world record attempt. However we can't start thinking about the performance right from the outset. There are many different ways of adding diversity. freediving amongst underwater wrecks in total silence allows you to experience the stories that they seem to tell.

(above)
Head of Ulysses, a fragment from a group of Hellenistic sculptors discovered in the Shrine of Tiberius (Sperlonga, National Archaeological Museum of Italy). Israeli and American scientists discovered a connection between DNA and the spirit of adventure, by researching the attributes of a group of volunteers. This genetic component was aptly called the 'Ulysses factor.'

It is important to note that this doesn't mean that the destiny of man, whether explorer or desk clerk, is all written in his DNA. Long years of study on identical twins has lead scientists to the conclusion that genes can account for only about 50% of the differences between people. The other half depends on the circumstances of life: family, culture, level of education, diet during infancy and thousands of other factors.

"The particular structure of this gene explains about 10% of the spirit of adventure," was a clarification made by the research department in the Herzog hospital of Jerusalem. "It might seem like a small amount, but in reality it is very significant. To make a comparison, if a scientist one day found a gene that explained one tenth of human intelligence it would be a sensational discovery. Granted, we have only explained 10% of this particular behaviour, but we are already working to locate the other genes which together make up the mosaic of the spirit of adventure."

There is then an invisible connection that crosses the centuries, uniting the 'extremists.' From Ulysses to Marco Polo, from Stathis Haggi to Enzo Maiorca, from Christopher Columbus to Bruno Peyron: each of them wanted to find out what was behind the line of the horizon, or over the next hilltop, and was almost condemned to do so. It was written in their genetic make-up. Personally I am also convinced that the spirit of adventure has a genetic component, but I refuse to believe that it can explain everything, or that it is paramount. These genetic predispositions must be combined with adaptation to the setting. Like all living things, man has at least two ways of adapting: the first is the sum total of all the attributes that allow him to survive in his natural habitat, for example intelligence, imagination, creativity and the

ability to communicate – in brief, everything that allows him to take advantage of the world around in order to better conduct his own life and improve the quality of his existence. The second consists in one or more attributes that are useful only in certain circumstances or environments that are very distinct from the natural environment, such as the blood shift that occurs during a deep freedive.

Of course the environmental factor plays an important role: persons encountered, education from parents, external stimuli and all other formative events and experiences have their part to play in determining behaviour. Especially when we are children the experiences and events of our lives shape our futures and give an irreversible direction to our existence. Nevertheless the writer and anthropologist Carlos Castaneda maintains that only he who challenges and overcomes the four natural enemies of man can aspire to reach the most authentic way of life. The four enemies are: Fear, which dethrones mental clarity; Clarity itself which blinds and hinders learning and hopes; Power, which is the strongest, because it makes one cruel and capricious; Old Age, which takes away the time to act.

We mustn't therefore be content with the natural ability that DNA grants us. The 'Ulysses Factor' can only emerge if it is extracted by the spirit of man and his freedom. It is not a privilege reserved to the elite, and it is manifested more often than we know. Many men and women experience and seek out extreme situations in their day to day life: driving at high speed for the thrilling sensation of the risk; constantly changing work in order to seek out novelty and unpredictability – in general taking on everything which allows us to evade the routine of an ordinary life, and being stimulated by that which would frighten anyone else. Even in this type of behaviour the 'Ulysses Factor' is manifested. But the first No Limits action taken by the species was millions of years ago: man, who was living peacefully in the trees, decided one day to come down to earth, to widen his horizons, affronting the perils and uncertainties of a new type of life.

Without the 'Ulysses Factor' mankind would probably still be blissfully hanging from the vines of the forest, or even further backwards in evolution. Life as we know it wouldn't exist. Time wouldn't exist.

The words of the writer Antonio Soccol summarise well this irrepressible urge: "Everything has a limit except for mankind. It is essential to man's existence that he continues to surpass himself, and therefore doesn't accept any limits. Freedom, the real uniqueness of our species, cannot tolerate conditions. It can never give up on any goal or desire." That is the reason why I freedive!

"Remember," my coach Massimo Giudicelli used to say, "you can only go so far as the sea lets you. Don't ever become complacent, but don't ever talk yourself down. Stay concentrated. If you win today enjoy the victory, but tomorrow start looking ahead again."

Freedivers establish an intimate bond with the sea. You talk to it, and confide in it. Sometimes you may even become angry with the sea, to the point of hating it. But in the end you will always make peace with the sea, because you know that without it you could not exist.

The history of freediving records

To relive the dawn of deep freediving we have to turn the clock back almost a hundred years.

In 1912, one year before Haggi performed his historic salvage of the Margherita's anchor, a Hungarian was born who would later become an Italian citizen and go on to establish the first official freediving world record: Raimondo Bucher. In 1949, when he announced that he would pass a parchment enclosed in a metal cylinder, as if it was the baton in a relay race, to a diver who would be standing on the muddy bottom of a 30 meter deep lake in Naples, scientists declared that this mad captain of the air force would certainly die from the crushing pressure.

Bucher wouldn't listen: he completed the dive, and became the 'world's deepest man.' He later admitted that he had attempted the depth for a wager made with the same diver who was waiting on the bottom: he won 50,000 lira, which in 1949 was a considerable sum. Bucher remained the 'deepest man' in the world for two years, until 1951 when, also in Naples, Ennio Falco and Alberto Novelli both descended to 35 meters. Bucher waited only one year before in Capri, 1952, he reclaimed the record with a 39 meter dive. At this time waterproof cases for cine cameras had just been invented, and Bucher's 39 meters constituted the first record documented on film.

The equipment that Raimondo Bucher used is very interesting. His snorkel was a piece of gas piping. The mask was rudimental, with a capacious internal volume, and equalising started to get difficult already at about ten meters. Not to mention the flippers, which, being made of very soft rubber, supplied a pitiful amount of force. Moreover the blade of the fin itself was very small – at the time freedivers used fins only slightly longer than their feet.

In 1956 Falco and Novelli returned to the stage, setting a new world record of 41 meters at Rapallo. After another interval of four years news arrived from Brazil that Americo Santarelli had reached 43 meters in Rio de Janeiro. 1960 was a year for records: Santarelli came to Italy and in the waters of Cape Circeo touched a depth of 44 meters. Soon after at Syracuse, Enzo Maiorca, the man who would dominate the history of freediving for the next thirty years, descended to 45 meters. Americo Santarelli moved to Santa Margherita Ligure and superseded this with 46. The unphased Maiorca promptly put three meters between himself and the Brazilian with a dive to 49 meters, still in his home waters. Then in 1961, for the first time, Enzo reached the milestone of 50 meters. "Don't go any deeper, because beyond 50 meters you'll be crushed," were the words of the French doctor Cabarrou. The Sicilian ignored Cabarrou's warning, and in 1962 at Ustica he moved the mark to 51 meters.

Science was resoundingly contradicted. Who can imagine Maiorca's state of mind as he set out from the surface on his way to beyond 50 meters, with all the world's medical theory against him. In such circumstances the greatness of the man is revealed.

Americo Santarelli retired, and Maiorca, now bereft of adversaries, registered 53 meters in Syracuse, August of 1964, and 54 meters in Acireale the following July. The peace for Maiorca lasted only a year however; in 1965 three new adversaries appeared on the scene: Teteke Williams, Robert "Bob" Croft, and Jacques Mayol.

A journalist of the time described these three athletes as thunderbolts in Maiorca's clear sky: the first a thunderclap, the second a raging storm, and the third a devastating hurricane.

Until this time CMAS (the World Confederation of Subaquatic Activities) had validated all the records. However the arrival of the new contenders coincided with more severe regulations: Williams' 59 meterdive in Polynesia, September 1965, Mayol's 60 meters in the Bahamas, June 1966, and the 64 meters of Croft in Florida, February 1967, weren't accepted as valid, even though they were entered directly into the archives of freediving.

Two photos of Raimondo Bucher, one of the key figures of deep freediving. Bucher continued freediving and scuba diving regularly into his nineties, and conducted a lot of important scientific research in the waters of Sardinia.

(both)
Ennio Falco during the practice of his favourite hobbies: spearfishing and diving for coral. He was distinguished for his grace and elegance underwater. As a demonstration of their close friendship, he attempted all his records together with Alberto Novelli.
These two men passed the flag to the Brazilian Amerigo Santarelli, considered by many as the strongest athlete in the history of freediving.

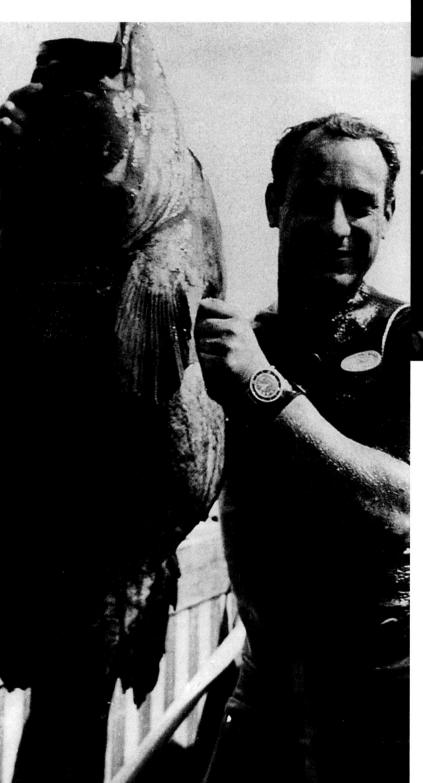

Nevertheless, Enzo Maiorca wasn't to be caught resting on his laurels, and in November of 1966 he descended to 62 meters in the waters of Syracuse, with all the proper officials. However the fact that Croft had already reached 64 meters wasn't to his liking, and in Cuba, inSeptember of 1967, he descended to the same depth.

Their techniques were very different. Croft, gifted with an impressive lung volume (nine and a half litres!) would dive naked of equipment – without fins or mask – and ascended by pulling himself up the guide rope. Mayol introduced the technique of yoga and mental concentration in an attempt to make up for a physique that wasn't exactly comparable to Tarzan!

As for Maiorca, commitment and determination constituted the basic elements of his style of diving 'headlong into the blue'. Croft, who evidently didn't attach much importance to CMAS, persisted with his records: in December of 1967 he reached 67 meters cleanly in Florida, but scarcely a month later, and also in Florida, the Shanghai-born Frenchman Jacques Mayol touched 70 meters. The American responded in August of 1968 with a handsome 73 meters. As far as CMAS was concerned it was all wasted effort, as they did not validate any of these performances. Croft was forced to leave the scene due to a pulmonary emphysema. Yet there was enough incentive to take Enzo Maiorca to 72 meters, and just a year later, still in the waters of Ognina, to 74 meters. A single month passed before Mayol reached 75 and straight after 76 meters in Japan.

On the 5th of December 1970, following a very serious decision from their medical commission, CMAS announced that they would no longer be validating any freediving records. One of the reasons they gave was the danger to the supporting scuba divers. For CMAS these performances were of scientific interest

only, and the confederation gave them an academic, but worthless acknowledgement as experiments. Mayol took sides with the research. Maiorca initially didn't want anything to do with it, but in the end ceded to the spirit of competition.

Inflamed by the 76 of Mayol, Maiorca descended past him into the abyss to 77 meters. He would repeat the feat with punctuality at Ognina and Genoa in the Augusts of the next two years, taking the baton to 78 and 80 meters. Mayol decided to move the challenge to the home of his rival, and in 1973 he appeared on the island of Elba, where he surpassed the Sicilian by a good six meters.

The reaction of Maiorca was almost immediate, and the next year he chose Sorrento as a venue to give a definite lesson to his rival: on the 22nd of September, 1974 Enzo was ready to attempt 90 meters. He ended up falling well short of that mark when he collided with one of the scuba divers, Enzo Bottesini, 18 meters

A photo from the sixties, with Maiorca (right) and Mayol (left) in the company of one of their fans. This was the beginning of their rivalry, which would continue for almost twenty years.

below the surface. Bottesini was hampered by a huge video camera and a mask that allowed him to speak underwater, and the current had pushed him against the rope down which Maiorca was quickly descending.

On Saturday the 28th of September, away from the chaos of the preceding Sunday, he had another try, and after hyperventilating for 10 minutes he descended to 87 meters. Two minutes and thirty six seconds later he was back on the surface, but unconscious, with a mouth full of frothy blood. It would take four minutes before the doctors could bring him round. Some of the onlookers were already grieving. When Enzo regained consciousness he looked up and asked, "So how did it go?"

The following year Mayol, still at Elba, flew down to 92 meters, and thirteen months later on the 23rd of November 1976 he reached the mythical depth of 101 meters. The records of the two great rivals in these years had a back-wash of controversy that gave little honour to the discipline of freediving. Mayol maintained that he didn't brave the abyss to set records, but for means of medical research only. His Sicilian rival rebutted that if Mayol really only wanted to carry out experiments then he would only need to bring his team of scuba divers and medics, without all the additional television crews, photographers, press, judges, officials and sponsors.

In 1983 Jacques Mayol touched 105 meters, and in 1988, at Syracuse, Enzo Maiorca also exceeded the momentous threshold, taking his mark to 101 meters – a fitting finish for a huge sporting career.

In these forty years of freediving history the equipment also underwent a remarkable evolution. The masks were packed with silicon to reduce their internal volume, making it easier to equalise them, and they were subsequently replaced with contact lenses.

With the current depths there are two main systems: you can either descend with bare eyes (like most of the South American freedivers) or you can use contact lenses, or lenses mounted in fluid-filled swimming goggles. For my attempts I used contact lenses with an optical power of two hundred diopters (the corrective power of everyday contact lenses ranges from

one to ten), and these allowed me to see in the water just like I was wearing a mask. The little rubber fins were also abandoned to make way for longer and more rigid designs. These days fins used in competitions reach almost a meter in length, and in the most sophisticated cases are fashioned from carbon fibre. The monofin has by now replaced the traditional 'bi-fins' as the most common equipment used in competitions.

Constant Weight has an equally rich and fascinating history. This discipline requires that the athlete descends and ascends under their own force, without touching the line and without releasing the weight belt that was used for the descent.

With these rules, the first to set a record of 50 meters was Stefano Makula (an Italian of Hungarian origin like Bucher) who opened a personal challenge in 1978 with Enzo Maiorca and his two pupils Nuccio and Mario Imbesi. The brothers both reached 52 meters in September of 1978, but in the same month Maiorca swam down to 55 meters. In 1979 Makula equalled Maiorca, even if in the same year they were both superseded by Enzo Liistro, who reached 56 meters. In June of 1980 Nuccio Imbesi moved the mark to 57 meters. Sixteen months passed before Makula descended to 58 meters in October of 1981. But all was not over: in November of the same year, Mayol (who else!) was the first to break the 60 meter barrier, with a dive to 61 meters.

Another year passed in relative peace amongst the world's deepest, with the exception of some sporadic appearances from Makula, first with Constant Weight dives and then with Variable Weight. However his attempts were never validated, until in 1988 in Giannutri his dive to 102 meters in Variable Weight was officially confirmed. The next year, on the 23rd of October in Ponza, he had a serious accident in an attempt to reach 110 meters.

Meanwhile word began circulating in Europe of a very strong Cuban apneist by the name of Francisco 'Pipin' Ferreras, who all the divers of the Caribbean were talking about with an almost reverent awe. They spoke of his de-

(above)
A portrait of Pipin.

(on the next page)
The Cuban athlete
ascending from a
Variable Weight
dive. The rivalry
between Pipin and
I monopolised the
world of freediving for
the whole decade of
the 1990's. It was often
compared to the epic
rivalry of the preceding
years between Mayol
and Maiorca. Pipin
associated with the
school of Maiorca, and
used the same safety
team. He borrowed
ideas of physical
training and muscular
force from Enzo, but
I was moulded by the
teachings of Mayol:
physically less powerful
than Pipin, but more
mentally prepared, I
was able to draw on
some of Jacques' old
team members for my
record attempts.

scent in Constant Weight to 67 meters in the autumn of 1987 and of a successive 69 meters in 1988, in the waters of Key Largo. These performances were never validated though, as he would ascend by pulling on the line, which was strictly forbidden by the regulations. It was in 1989 at Key Largo that I first met Pipin.

Then came a very important year for freediving. The friendly Frenchman Frank Messegué reached 62 meters in Constant Weight at Reunion island, reopening the record books in this discipline eight years after Mayol's 61 meters. Pipin began practicing the discipline of Variable Weight, and in Cuba on the 3rd of November 1989 he plummeted down to 112 meters, earning for the first time the title of 'world's deepest man'.

At this point an adjustment was made. The Italian Federation of 1989 (one of the few world federations that continued to recognise freedives after the veto of CMAS) created a new set of directives. Constant weight wasn't affected – the athlete still had to descend and ascend under their own force, without touching the guideline – but several rules of Variable

Weight were changed. Following the new ruling, an athlete could use a ballast of no more than one third of their bodyweight to achieve maximum depth, and the ballast would be left on the bottom while the athlete ascended under their own power. The use of lift bags or inflatable wetsuits was no longer allowed.

These two disciplines of constant and Variable Weight were officially recognised by the Federation, whilst the category of 'No Limits', (the old Variable Weight practised by Mayol and Maiorca in which the athlete descends with unlimited ballast and returns to the surface by means of an inflated lift bag), was no longer recognised, although it was still 'officialised' by the presence of CMAS judges. Thus we resume the story, with Messegué's 62 meters for Constant Weight, the 87 meters of Maiorca for Variable Weight and Pipin's 112 meters in No Limits.

In September of 1990, several months after having achieved 112 meters, and after transferring to Maiorca's own Sicily, Pipin took the record in Constant Weight from 62 to 63 meters, and that of Variable Weight from 87 to 92 meters. This was the moment that I entered into the game.

On the 11th of November 1990, in the waters of Porto Azzurro, I set my first world record in the discipline of Constant Weight, taking the mark down to 65 meters. From this day forth, Pipin and I began a great rivalry, which has often been compared to that of Mayol and Maiorca of the preceding years. In 1991 Pipin failed in an attempt at Constant Weight before improving his No Limits depth to 115 meters, on the 6th of July.

In October of the same year, and still at Port Azzurro, I answered back, establishing world records in all three disciplines in the course of one month: on the 2nd, 22nd and 26th of October I reached 67 meters in Constant Weight, 95 meters in Variable Weight and 118 meters in No Limits.

In May of 1992, on his own island of Varadero, Pipin took my most cherished record, Constant Weight, with a dive to 68 meters. It was only for a few months though: on the 17th of September I went two metres deeper to 70 meters during the Blue Olympiad at Ustica.

In the course of the same event Pipin, first attempting 101 meters in Variable Weight but surfacing with a blackout, went onto avenge himself with 120 meters in No Limits on the 20th of September. Pipin persisted in Variable Weight, and, after abandoning the idea of 101 meters, he surpassed me by a single meter to take the record to 96 meters.

On the 11th of October in the waters of Montecristo, and after much delay due to bad weather, I reclaimed the title of 'deepest man' with a depth of 123 meters in No Limits. But just one month later on the 12th of November in Freeport, Bahamas Pipin descended to 125 meters. He improved on this depth three more times: in Sicily in July of 1994 with 126 meters, in November of the same year in Florida with 127 meters and on the 30th of July 1995, back in Syracuse with 128 meters.

At the end of 1993 a group of French scuba divers, medics, technicians and apneists created AIDA (International Association for the Development of Apnea) whose purpose was to regulate and standardise freediving world record attempts. AIDA now forms the greatest refereeing body in the sport. Since 1994 they have been present at almost all official attempts at an international level.

On the 26th of July at Cala Gonone in Sardinia, I succeeded in Variable Weight where Pipin had failed two years before in Ustica: going five meters deeper than the Cuban to take the mark to 101 meters. I improved on this on the 22nd of July the following year, with a depth of 105 meters. Six days earlier on the 16th of July I had set a new Constant Weight record of 72 meters, in the course of the same event in Villasimius, a village close to Cagliari in Sardinia.

At the end of September 1995 Eric Charrier, a Corsican of thirty-three years, attempted 73 meters. Unfortunately he had a problem during the ascent that required the intervention of surface support, something that is categorically prohibited by the rules that validate attempts. The press release stated, "Upon reaching the surface, Eric Charrier was already unconscious. Within a few seconds he was taken onboard the support boat where he was administered with oxygen. He regained consciousness after about a minute."

On the 15th of December 1995, under the presidency of Achille Ferrero, CMAS made a change that surprised everyone: to review their decision of the 5th of December 1970 and resume the recognition and validation of freediving records, although limited solely to Constant Weight. It was an important decision that rewarded the most demanding and authentic of the three sporting categories. The rules for Constant Weight remained unchanged, and from 1996 this discipline was once again officially recognised in the hundred or so countries that support CMAS.

In this season of 1996 two new crusaders stepped into the limelight: the Italian Gianluca Genoni, who had been my safety freediver for years, and who achieved his first world record on the 17th of August with a Variable Weight dive to 106 meters, and the Frenchman Michel Oliva, a Corsican from Ile Rousse, who equalled my Constant Weight record of 72 meters in October.

In the meantime I was concentrating exclusively on the two disciplines with ballast, and in the space of a week between the 9th and the 16th of September I re-conquered the records of Variable Weight, with 110 meters, and No Limits, with 131 meters. But the season wasn't finished yet: about a month later in Nice the first freediving world teams championships were organised. I was too tired to participate as an athlete, so I decided to coach the Italian team, consisting of a group of young freedivers who were keen to make a big impression in their first international event. Surprising everyone, Italy won this first edition of the championships, ahead of the other eight teams on total points.

A few months after my 131 meters No Limits record, Pipin surpassed me with a brilliant 133 meters. The year of 1997 didn't start so well for me. The Cuban Alejandro Ravelo, in his international debut, took both my Constant Weight record (73 meters) and Variable Weight record (111 meters), exceeding me by a meter in both disciplines. All this happened in the waters of Syracuse, Sicily, and they were using the well-oiled team that had followed Enzo Maiorca during his records.

(above)
Here I am with Gianluca Genoni, in a photo taken in 1995 after my Constant Weight world record. At that point Gianluca was still part of my safety team.

(below)
A photo of Michel Olivia. He was definitely one of the strongest French freedivers, and a formidable adversary in the Constant Weight discipline.

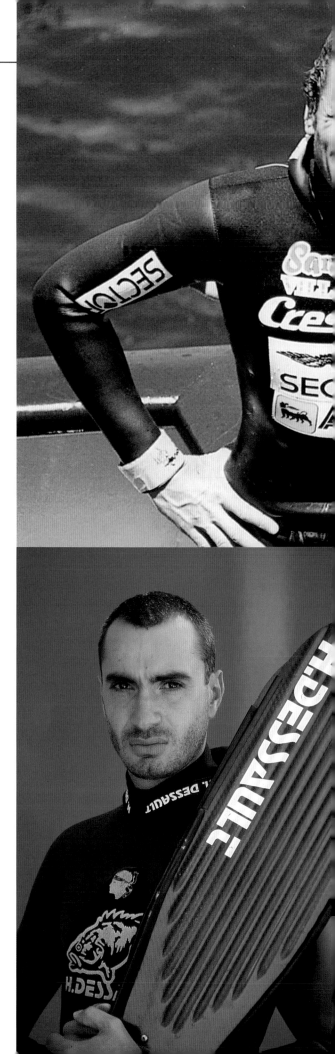

I wasn't about to give up though – quite the opposite! The idea of not owning any world records anymore motivated me, and in September of the same year at Porto Venere I claimed the Constant Weight title with 75 meters, and Variable Weight with 115 meters. Ravelo tried to get the Variable Weight record back straight away, but his attempt during the winter in Miami ended in failure. In July of 1998 he was back in Syracuse, to have a go at the Constant Weight record. He was quite obviously unconscious when he surfaced from 76 meters, but his attempt was validated by CMAS all the same. This created pandemonium in the Italian freediving scene, and everyone was asking me when I would be back in the water to 'teach the Cuban a lesson.' I told them I would wait until the following year in order to make it more decisive. In the meantime, I was training for the second edition of the freediving world teams championships, which were to be held at Santa Teresa di Gallura, with over thirty-five participating nations. This time I was competing as an ath-

(below)
Here I am with Gaspare Battaglia (center) and Davide Carrera (left). The first is a humble athlete but with incredible determination, and great staying power – it was Gaspare who lead Italy to victory at the world championships in Ibiza. Davide is without doubt the most elegant and aquatic freediver that I have ever seen in the water.

lete in the Italian team, and once again we established ourselves as the strongest freediving nation, leaving our eternal rivals, the French, in second position.

In 1998 I didn't attempt any world records since I was occupied with a very different kind of a dive on the Island of Karpathos in Greece. Without any equipment (no mask, wetsuit or fins), I was pulled down by a heavy stone to the sea bottom 100 meters below, in the same way that the Greek sponge fishermen had dived a century before me. During this time Gianluca Genoni claimed the records in the sled disciplines, with 120 meters in Variable Weight and 135 meters in No Limits in Porto Ottiolu, Sardinia. A year later a new French diver, Loïc Leferme from Nice, took the No Limits title

(above)
The Venezuelan Carlos Coste, one of the few athletes to have set records in both Constant Weight and Variable Weight, in a time when most freedivers concentrate on one of the two.

(left)
Herbert Nitsch, an incredible Austrian athlete, with the strength and determination of a champion. He has dominated the men's freediving scene in recent years.

from Genoni, with 137 meters, but within a few weeks Genoni reclaimed it with a 138 meter dive.

It seemed like the season was over for 1999, but that wasn't quite the case: I hadn't forgotten my promise from the year before to take away Ravelo's undeserved record in Constant Weight, and so in the waters of Portofino, during one of the worst weeks of weather for the year, I claimed an unforgettable double: on the 18th of October I moved the Constant Weight world record to 80 meters, and six days later

took the record to 150 meters in No Limits.

With this second dive I had broken the world record by twelve meters: Maiorca was the first to reach 50 meters, Mayol broke the 100 meter barrier, and I was the first to 150.

In 2000 I didn't attempt any records, since I was involved in the filming of the Imax movie Ocean Men, that featured Pipin and I.

In 2001 I decided to take part in the third edition of the Freediving World Teams Championships, this time in Ibiza, Spain, with over forty nations competing. Italy won for the third consecutive time, beating France by only a handful of points. I decided to close my sporting career with the discipline of Variable Weight, which I had been unable to attempt in 1999 due to the poor weather conditions. Genoni had managed to shift the record by five meters over four seasons, and the mark to beat was 126 meters. On the 3rd of November 2001, in Capri, I broke the record by five meters, with a Variable Weight dive to 131 meters. When I got out of the water I announced that I had officially ended my record-breaking career.

The world freediving scene has by now completely changed. The dualism between Pipin and I that defined the challenge of freediving in the 1990's has been replaced by a completely new reality.

The use of the monofin has given way to huge leaps in the discipline of Constant Weight, and all recent records in this discipline have been set by the Austrian Herbert Nitsch, the Czech Martin Stepanek, Frenchman Guillaume Nery and the Venezuelan Carlos Coste. They surpass each other several times a year, and the record in Constant Weight has now passed to the incredible depth of 124 meters. Italy has slipped behind the other nations a little, but is well represented by Federico Mana, who was the first Italian to exceed the 100 meter mark, and

Davide Carrera. Ryuzo Shinomiya from Japan, William Trubridge and Dave Mullins from New Zealand, Alexey Molchanov from Russia, Manolis Giankos from Greece and Walter Steyn from Australia have all passed the 100 meter mark also.

In Variable Weight the main protagonists have been Carlos Coste and Martin Stepanek, but Herbert Nitsch recently left his mark on this discipline also, and the world record has crept out beyond 140 meters.

No Limits continues to be the most dangerous freediving discipline, and in 2007 Frenchman Loïc Leferme drowned tragically when his equipment failed during a training dive for a planned record attempt. Two freedivers have now exceeded the incredible depth of 200 meters, and they have both had to adopt new and demanding equalising techniques to counter the crushing pressures. Patrick Musimu was the first to cross the 200 meter threshold, flooding his sinuses and middle ears with water in order to descend to 209 meters on the 30th June, 2005. Herbert Nitsch followed in June, 2007, with a dive to 214 meters, using an even more revolutionary technique: he begins his dive equipped with a plastic bottle (which is obviously filled with water, not air), which he proceeds to fill with air from his lungs at a depth of 30 meters. He continues the dive with half-empty lungs, and when he is unable to equalise any deeper he begins to retrieve the air from the bottle in order to equalise to incredible depths. In this way the air from the bottle can be sent straight to the ears without having to be taken

(above)
Guillaume Nery, an elegant athlete, is the youngest of the top performing freedivers, setting his first world record in Constant Weight at the age of twenty two years. In France he is talked about as the future Jacques Mayol.

(left)
Martin Stepanek, who says that he was drawn to freediving after watching a film about Pipin and I. Originally from the Czech Republic, Martin lives, trains and teaches in Florida, where he has opened his own freediving school.

(with enormous difficulty) from the lungs. Both athletes are planning even deeper dives. In coming years these equalisation techniques may allow for man reach the dizzying depth of 300 meters.

In recent years a new discipline has emerged, Constant Weight Without Fins, where the athlete descends and ascends without touching the rope, and using only their own hands and feet for propulsion, swimming a kind of adapted underwater breaststroke. After its inclusion into the official disciplines of AIDA in 2004

numerous freedivers have taken up the challenge of this fascinating specialty: Martin Stepanek's 80 meter world record in April 2005 lasted a full two years before the New Zealander William Trubridge claimed the record on April 11th, 2007, with a dive to 81 meters in Dean's Blue Hole on Long Island in the Bahamas. Since then he has broken the record another nine times, most recently with a 101 meter no fins freedive in December of 2010 – a record that will be remembered in the history books in times to come.

Bottom left: the New Zealander William Trubridge, first man in the world to reach the depth of 100 meters in constant weight with no fins.

Bottom right: the Belgium Patrick Musimu, first man to break the 200 meter barrier in No Limits.

The women freedivers

The history of women's freediving began in the early 1960's. On the 26th of July, 1965, twenty-one year old Giuliana 'Jolly' Treleani dove to 31 meters, taking the title of 'deepest woman' that was established with a 30 meter dive the previous year by Hedy Roessler, who in her turn had overtaken the 25 meters of Francesca Trombi.

A few months later the English girl Evelyn Petterson descended to 33 meters in the Bahamas, but Giuliana reclaimed the record with 35 meters at Eolie on the 24th of July 1966.

Petterson responded with 38 meters, again in the Bahamas. Giuliana travelled to Cuba together with Enzo Maiorca, and reached 45 meters. These were all records in Variable Weight, but at this time in Cuba the sister of Treleani, Maria, descended to 31 meters in Constant Weight.

The Maiorca sisters, daughters of Enzo, appeared on the scene in 1978, with Patrizia straight away setting a record in Constant Weight. The next year her sister Rossana caught up to her, and together they went down to 40 meters.

In 1980 Patrizia suspended her diving due to pregnancy, but her sister Rossana continued

Rossana Maiorca, who left a unforgettable mark on Italian freediving. Together with her father Enzo Maiorca, she attempted world records during their "Operation Pythagoras."

Angela Bandini with Jacques Mayol in a photo from the end of the 1980's. Angela shocked the world when for the first time in the history of freediving she broke a men's world record, and she was the first female freediver to break the 100 meter barrier. The most amazing thing about her was her tiny physique: no one could understand how someone so small could stand up to the immense pressure of the depths. She had a lung volume of little more than three liters.

For a while Tanya Streeter held both the men's and women's No Limits world record, with a dive of 160 meters. This still stands as the women's world record today. Thanks to her talent and efforts, freediving has become a well-known sport in the United States and the Caribbean.

Deborah Andollo monopolised the world of women's freediving for years with her fantastic records. Along with Pipin, she was the greatest product of the Cuban school of freediving, which with the French and Italians was traditionally one of the strongest nations in the sport.

alone to 45 meters. There followed six long years of quiet, until in 1986 Rossana joined her father in the waters of Crotone for Operation Pythagoras, a series of experimental dives that concluded with a new women's record in Variable Weight of 69 meters.

In 1987 the Maiorca sisters returned to the waters of Syracuse: Patrizia surpassed her sister's Variable Weight record by a meter, with a 70 meter dive, while Rossana exceeded Patrizia by five meters in Constant Weight. In 1988, and again in Syracuse for 'Operation Aretusa,' Patrizia matched her 70 meters, while Rossana reached 80.

One year later Angela Bandini, a twenty-eight year old student of Mayol from Rimini, trounced everyone, men included, with 107 meters in No Limits. From 1990 to 1993 there was only Rossana Maiorca, who dedicated herself exclusively to the discipline of Constant Weight, taking the record to 59 metres, a depth that surpassed the personal best of her father, Enzo. The next year she decided to retire in order to dedicate herself to her family.

At this point there were no Italian heroines on the world freediving scene. The queen was

undoubtedly the Cuban Deborah Andollo, championess of synchronized swimming, who had been in her national team for twelve years. In a short time she also took herself to the top of freediving with dives to 67 meters in Constant Weight, 95 in Variable Weight and 115 meters in No Limits.

In Sardinia, in September 1998, Tanya Streeter made her debut in the blue arena of the world's deepest women, with 67 meters in Constant Weight. Tanya specialised in the hardest and purest discipline, Constant Weight, reaching 70 meters. She then turned to the sled disciplines, and between 2002 and 2003 she set world records of 160 meters in No Limits and 122 meters in Variable Weight, both in the waters of the Turks and Caicos islands.

The Canadian Mandy Rae Cruickshank was the first to break Tanya's Constant Weight world record, with 78 meters in the Cayman Islands in 2004. Then in September 2005 the Russian woman Natalia Molchanova set the first of many world records, with an incredible dive to 86 meters at the AIDA World Championships in Nice. The English-born Sara Campbell, who broke

Sara Campbell, often called 'Mighty Mouse' on account of her small stature (she is just under 5 feet tall). She broke into the freediving scene in 2007 and set her first world record only six months later.

Mandy-Rae Cruickshank, a Canadian athlete who has been one of the top female freedivers of recent years. She retired to raise a family, after 12 national records and 7 world records across multiple disciplines. She is undoubtedly one of the more elegant athletes that freediving has been graced with.

her first world record a year after learning how to freedive, has been the only challenger to Natalia's crown. In 2007 she dove to 90 meters in Dahab, Egypt. Natalia replied the following year with 95 meters in Crete, Greece. Then in 2009 Sara broke back with 96 meters in Dean's Blue Hole, in the Bahamas. Days later she attempted a 100 meter dive, but failed by a narrow margin – blacking out on the surface at the end of the dive, with the tag in her hand. Later in the same year Natalia was the first woman to make this historic depth, with a magnificent dive to 101 meters in Sharm el Sheikh, Egypt, but unfortunately it wasn't classified as a world record, since there weren't adequate official judges present.

Natalia Molchanova has prevailed over the Constant Weight Without Fins discipline as well, setting a world record of 55 meters in Dahab, Egypt, in 2005. Sara Campbell and Russian Natalie Avseenko each added a meter in 2007 and 2008, but since then the discipline has been dominated by Natalia Molchanova, who has moved the world record to the current mark of 62 meters, set at the 2009 AIDA World Championships in the Bahamas.

The Russians, Natalia Molchanova and her son Alexey. Natalia is the undisputed queen of freediving: she was the first to exceed 100 meters in constant weight, and has set world records in almost all the specialties. Her son, Alexey is one of the rising stars on the world circuit. He is already very strong in dynamic apnea (having set a world record of 250 meters), and is poised to join the ranks of the top in the depth disciplines also. He has a very refined style, and an innate aquaticity.

Umberto Pelizzari's records

Constant Weight

The athlete reaches maximum depth using only the force of his legs, and returns in the same way, without ever touching the descent line.

Variable Weight

The athlete uses a sled, with a weight that cannot exceed 30 kilograms, to reach maximum depth. The sled is left at the bottom and the athlete ascends under their own force without the use of any kind of auxiliary such as a lift bag.

-65 meters	Elba island	1990		-95 meters	Elba island	1991
-67 meters	Elba island	1991		-101 meters	Cala Gonone	1994
-70 meters	Ustica	1992		-105 meters	Villasimius	1995
-72 meters	Villasimius	1995		-110 meters	Villasimius	1996
-75 meters	Portovenere	1997		-115 meters	Portovenere	1997
-80 meters	Portofino	1999		-131 meters	Capri	2001

No Limits

In this discipline the athlete reaches maximum depth using a sled with no weight restrictions. The return to the surface can be achieved using a lift bag.

"... do you know what you're supposed to do,
to meet a mermaid?
You go down to the bottom of the sea,
where the water isn't even blue anymore,
where the sky is only a memory,
and you float there, in the silence.
And you stay there,
and you decide that you'll die for them.
Only then do they start coming out.
They come, and they greet you,
and they judge the love you have for them.
If it's sincere, if it's pure, they'll be with you,
and take you away forever."

Jacques Mayol from the film *The Big Blue*, 1988

-118 meters	Elba island	1991
-123 meters	Montecristo	1993
-131 meters	Villasimius	1996
-150 meters	Portofino	1999

One last mouthful of earthly life
a reluctant departure from the sun

and then down, to glimpse
her unworldly lightness of being
and to admire her vitality

the sensuality of her caresses
the desire to belong to her

her power and strength
the heady urge to resist her

her immense silent form
the knowledge that it's yours

the boldness of her shapes
the danger of a pretentious lover

the clearness of her character
the respect for deep affection

not a contestant
nor a rival
nor an enemy

but an accomplice
a friend
a guest of honour

the fusion of two inseparable entities
YOU and YOUR sea

Finally you're back
… I missed you already

Stefania

Bibliography

AA.VV., La grande enciclopedia del mare, Armando Curcio Editore, Rome 1979

AA.VV., Manuale federale di immersione, La Mandragora, Imola 1994

F. Antonelli, A. Salvini, La psicologia dello sport, oggi, Società Stampa Sportiva, Rome 1977

J.P. Bonnin, C. Grimaud, J.-C. Happey, J.M. Strub, Plongée sous-marine et milieu subaquatique. Ac- cidents, aspects médi- caux, Masson Editeur, Paris 2003

J.H. Corriol, La plongée en apnée. Physiologie et médecine, Masson Editeur, Paris 2002

J. Cousteau, Les secrets d'une plongée, Hachette Jeunesse, Paris 1991

F. Ferreras, Gli abissi tutti d'un fiato, A&A, Milan 1991

X. Fructus, R. Sciarli, La plongée. Santé, securité, Ed. Ouest-France, Rennes 1992

J. Johnson, Michel Odent, We are all water babies, Celestial Arts 1995

E. Maiorca, A capofitto nel turchino, Mursia, Milan 1977

E. Maiorca, Sotto il segno di Tanit, Rizzoli, Milan 1980

J. Mayol, Apnea a meno 100, Fratelli Fabbri Editori, Milan 1976

J. Mayol, Homo Delphinus, Giunti Martello, Florence 1979

J. Mayol, Homo Delphinus, Idelson Gnocchi, Naples 2006

Ocean Men, BSV Burgschmiet Verlag, Nürnberg 2001

U. Pelizzari, L. Landoni, A. Seddone, Breathing in Breathold diving, Idelson Gnocchi, Naples 2011

U. Pelizzari, S. Tovaglieri, Corso di Apnea, Mursia, Milan 2001

U. Pelizzari, Il Respiro nell'Apnea, Mursia, Milan 2009

U. Pelizzari (with the collaboration of D. Menard), L'homme et la mer, Arthaud, Paris 2004

U. Pelizzari, S. Tovaglieri, Manual of Freediving, Idelson-Gnocchi, Naples 2004

G. Poulet, R. Barincou, La plongée, Editions Denoël, Paris 1984

G. Roghi, Uomini e pesci, Sperling & Kupfler, Milan 1977

C. Tedeschi, Angela degli abissi, Edizioni Dare, 1990

M. Thomere, Les liaisons dangereuses avec la mer, Editions Homme et perspectives, 1995

A. Van Lysebeth, Pranayama, la dynamique du souffle, Flammarion, 1993

Photographic credits

Manual of Freediving
Underwater on a single breath
by UMBERTO PELIZZARI and
STEFANO TOVAGLIERI
ISBN 192864927-0 - Softcover: 366 pages
$ 39,50 - € 35,00

From theory to practice: the first entirely illustrated and complete guide to freediving
The definitive guide, illustrated and up to date, for the aspiring apneist. From theory to practice this manual will accompany the reader in the discovery of a fascinating sport.
A manual that should not be missing from the itinerary of any diver (apneist or otherwise) who wishes to improve their techniques of respiration, swimming and diving whilst broadening knowledge and theory.
Dozens of exercises, illustrated with helpful sequences of pictures allow both student and instructors of apnea to follow a simple and effective teaching path.
From the experience of two sportsmen, with years dedicated to competitive and instructive apnea, finally a manual that unites theory with practical.

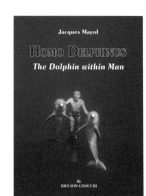

Homo Delphinus
The Dolphin Within Man
by JACQUES MAYOL
ISBN 192864903-3 - Hardcover: 398 pages
$ 95,00 - € 98,00

The only book written about Man's spiritual connection to the sea. The term Homo Delphinus refers to individuals who are aquatic as dolphin, share a love of the ocean. Mayol believed that some people will be, within a couple of generations, capable of swimming at depths of 200 meters and holding their breath for up to ten minutes.

This book is also a limited edition coffee-table size book includes more than 300 pictures.

The Ten Kings of the Sea
Salvage of Santa Isabella's Treasure
by JACQUES and PIERRE MAYOL
ISBN 192864924-6 - Softcover: 256 pages
$ 25,00 - € 19,50

A novel based on real discoveries and experiences made by Jacques Mayol around the world during his life who was dedicated to discovering the underwater secrets of the Sea.

Breatheology
the art of conscious breathing
by STIG ÅVALL SEVERINSEN
ISBN 192864934-3 - Softcover: 300 pages
$ 39,50 - € 35,00

"Those who breath half, live half"
(ACHARYA MILIND KUMAR BHARDWAY)

Most of us breathe inefficiently. Life is often lived in the fast lane, and especially when we are stressed, we tend to use only the upper part of our lungs. We forget to breathe deep down into the stomach and thereby lose out on a lot of energy.

Only when you become aware of your breathing and how to train it, you will be able to learn to breathe properly. Your body will immediately absorb more oxygen and after a short time you will have more energy and gain greater mental calmness.

The Mediterranean Diet
Origins and Myths
by DARIO GIUGLIANO, M.D.
ISBN: 192864911-4
Hardcover: 266 pages
$ 75,00

This book covers the origins, the history and the myths that have developed regarding the Mediterranean diet. It also applies scientific data and research to reveal the true benefits of the foods of this geographical region and their effects for healthy living. The research has come from ancient literature and contemporary medical studies and by archeological and historical discoveries from countries surrounding the Mediterranean Sea.

This book is a limited edition coffee-table size book includes more than 365 pictures.

forthcoming titles

Breathing
in breathold diving
by UMBERTO PELIZZARI
LISETTA LANDONI
and ANNA SEDDONE
ISBN 192864932-7

Red Gold
*"An account about the plunder
and protection of red coral off the coast of Sardinia,
that is in danger of extinction due to human intervention.
It covers extreme diving and Hyperbaric treatments."*
by LEONARDO FUSCO
ISBN 192864929 7
www.redcoralsociety.org

GG